ADIRONDACK ENIGMA

THE DEPRAVED INTELLECT & MYSTERIOUS LIFE OF NORTH COUNTRY WIFE KILLER HENRY DEBOSNYS

CHERI L. FARNSWORTH

THE
History
PRESS

Published by The History Press
Charleston, SC 29403
www.historypress.net

Copyright © 2010 by Cheri L. Farnsworth
All rights reserved

Cover design by Natasha Momberger

First published 2010

ISBN 9781540234827

Library of Congress Cataloging-in-Publication Data

Farnsworth, Cheri, 1963-
Adirondack enigma : the depraved intellect and mysterious life of North Country wife
killer Henry Debosnys / Cheri L. Farnsworth.
p. cm.
Includes bibliographical references and index.
ISBN 978-1-59629-868-2
1. Debosnys, Henry, d. 1883. 2. Murderers--New York (State)--Biography. 3. Murder-
-New York (State)--History--19th century. I. Title.
HV6248.D343F37 2010
364.152'3092--dc22
[B]
2009051624

I dedicate this book to my wonderful husband, Leland Farnsworth II, and four beautiful daughters—Jamie, Katie, Michelle and Nicole Revai. S'agapo, Je t'adore, I love you, Te amo, Eu te amo, Te quiero.

CONTENTS

Why do we vainly weep at fate
and sigh for life's uncertain date?
The light of gold can never illume
the drairy midnight of the tomb.

—Henry D. Debosnys

Prologue

I will both lay me down in peace, and sleep, and consider mine enemies: for they are many and speak evil about me. But my heart and my flesh will rejoice in the grave. I have seen all the work done under the sun. There is nothing but vanity and vexation of spirit. (Vidi cunctu, quae fiunt subsola, et ecce universa vanitas et afflictio spiritus.) To everything there is a season, and a time to every purpose under the heaven: there is a time to be born, and a time to die; a time to get, and a time to lose; a time to keep, and a time to cast away; a time to keep silence, and a time to speak; a time to love, and a time to hate; a time for war, and a time for peace; a time to mourn, and a time for the grave. At last we all go unto one place. We all are of the dust, and we all return to dust again.

I have considered all the oppressions that are done under the sun, and the tears of the oppressed, where is no comfort; but on the side of the oppressors, there is power called law. But it is no comfort. Speculation is the only comfort of the law for the oppressors, but not a comfort. So I praise the dead which are already dead, more than the living, which are yet alive. The dead fear no more the oppressors.

It is better to go to the house of mourning, than to go to the house of feasting: for that is the end of all men. The heart of the wise is in the house of mourning; but the heart of the fool is in the house of mirth—the house of the oppressors. Oh, the grave; there in the grave the oppressors are no more! In the grave the rich sleep with the poor, the king and the slave, the servant with the master. In the grave there is no more speculation; king, master, servant, slave, rich and poor go to the dust where there is no return, no more. Death has no remembrance. Truly, the light is sweet and pleasant to the eyes, but the grave is better for the spirit and body. There we leave all our troubles of this world for an eternal rest. There I will see wonders in the heavens and in the earth.

When blood, fire, pillars of smoke, earthquake and thunder; when the sun is turned into darkness and the moon into blood; when the stars shall withdraw their shining and the mountains sink down, and all the world be in a great desolation, then you will remember the great and terrible day that comes. On that day, if it be in my power, I will send to you the great fire of destruction, on the wall of your house which shall devour all the dwelling, and cut off the inhabitant, and many will die on that day of vengeance.

Those things will happen before many months. But you will remember that those few lines are from a big fool.

Henry Debosnys
Elizabethtown, Essex County, New York
April, III, MDCCCLXXXIII

ACKNOWLEDGEMENTS

Many thanks to my commissioning editor, Saunders Robinson; my project editor, Ryan Finn; and Emily Navarro from the production team at The History Press for signing me on and for your enthusiasm and interest in this project. To my husband, Leland, thank you for your unwavering support and great ideas (and for keeping me from getting lost out there). My girls—Nicole, Katie, Jamie and Michelle, thank you for helping me decide what to write about next and for having the forthrightness (Jamie, dear) to tell me that something I've written is too confusing or "messed up" and needs to be changed for clarity. (You were right, of course.) As always, thanks so much to my parents, Tom and Jean Dishaw, who instilled a love of written expression and creativity in all of their children (and grandchildren, come to think of it). To Cindy "C.J." Barry, Christina Walker and Tom Dishaw…I was truly blessed to have you three as my siblings. A big shout-out goes to *their* significant others (Ed, Rachel and Ryan Barry; Danon Hargadin; Bryan, Lindsey and little Cade Alexander Walker; and Heather and Amanda Walker) and to my in-laws, Carol and Lee Farnsworth.

Special thanks to Margaret Gibbs and Jenifer Kuba at the Adirondack History Center Museum and Brewster Library in Elizabethtown for being the conscientious keepers of Henry's skull, noose and the original works he created in jail (and for sharing a few good laughs on my visit, compliments of Henry, I'm sure); to my all-time favorite website, the Northern New York Historical Newspapers website, for offering a whopping 1.7 million pages from forty-four local newspapers online; and to Vicki Weiss of the New York

ACKNOWLEDGEMENTS

State Library in Albany for enthusiastically providing me with copies of comprehensive files relating to the Debosnys murder case from the library's Manuscripts and Special Collections Department (the Robert F. Hall Papers, SC21219). Thanks again to Jessie Olcott and Tom Scozzafava, who provided information regarding the Adirondack History Center Museum and the Essex County Government Center that I've used in two other books, as well as in this one.

INTRODUCTION

When Henry Deletnack Debosnys (so-called) arrived in Essex, New York, in the spring of 1882, he convinced a well-to-do, widowed mother of four to marry him, barely three months after burying his second wife, Celestine, in Philadelphia. Elizabeth "Betsey" Wells and Henry Debosnys were wed just five weeks after meeting each other, and she was dead—her throat slashed—two months into their surreptitious union. It was a sensational story that shook the North Country to its core. Witnesses placed Debosnys at the scene of the crime near Port Henry. From that moment on, he never stood a chance (deservedly so, some might exclaim)—not with a crime as shocking and heinous as his. He was tried, convicted of first-degree murder and sent to the old Essex County Jail in Elizabethtown to await execution by hanging. But if the citizens of Essex County thought Debosnys was nothing more than a crafty, opportunistic, wife-murdering gold-digger, they had another thought coming.

The enigmatic foreigner spent his entire incarceration feverishly penning his mysterious, seemingly extraordinary life in fluent Greek, French, English, Latin, Portuguese and Spanish, suggesting that he was not only a cold-blooded killer but also a highly educated polyglot, with an apparent gift of fabrication at that. Unless…unless his self-proclaimed biography were true and his background really was as extraordinary as he portrayed it to be. Regardless of the impressive resume he handily crafted, the abundance of death-themed sketches he produced in jail revealed a disturbed mind at work, and the poetry he crafted—while outwardly reasonable—was both morbid and telling when taken into context and carefully considered. It was

these natural abilities—the art, the storytelling and the poetry (in multiple languages)—that drew scores of sympathetic females to the jail to comfort the condemned man, deceived perhaps by his charm and obvious intellect, as Betsey Wells and others before her had been.

Although Debosnys took his true name to the grave, he insisted the answer to that puzzle lay in the unsolved ciphers he produced in jail. Thus, he was to nineteenth-century Northern New York what the Zodiac Killer was to twentieth-century Southern California: an arrogant murderer who left a deliberate trail of clues and cryptograms in his wake, daring us (even today) to identify him, if we think we have what it takes. In an age of easy access to online information like veterans' rosters, Freemasonry symbols, genealogical data and examples of every type of cipher and secret code ever used, we *do* have what it takes, at last. That's why, even though the events recorded here occurred more than a century ago, the time to solve the riddle of Henry Debosnys's life is now.

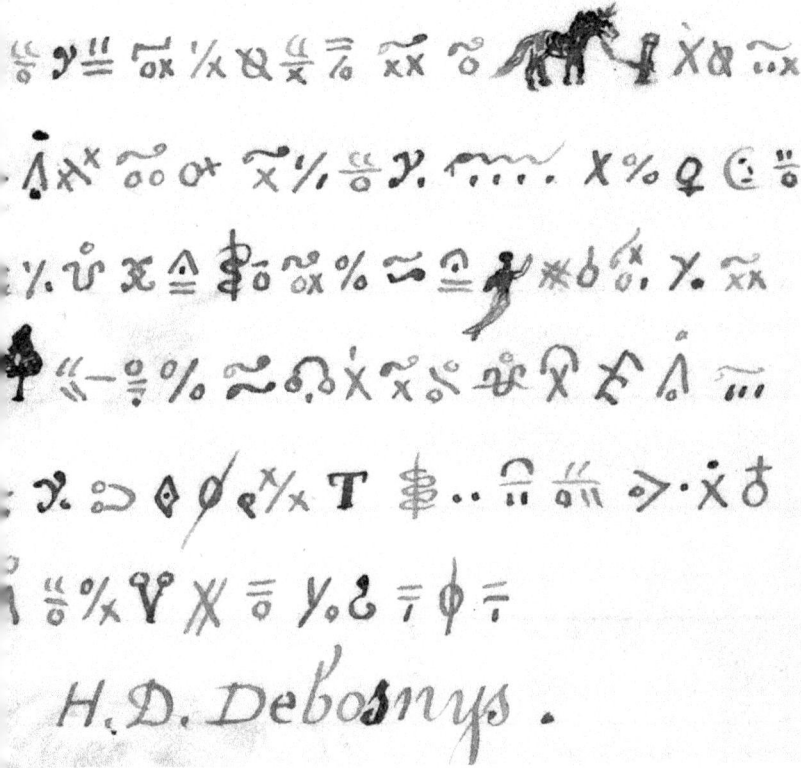

Debosnys self-portrait with cryptogram, created in jail. *Courtesy of the Collection of Brewster Memorial Library/ Essex County Historical Society.*

Within these pages is all you need to begin your search for the identity of the Adirondack's most famous (and, undoubtedly, most scholarly) convicted wife killer. Countless news articles are referenced—many with variations to the spelling of Debosnys's unusual name, as you'll see. I retyped the English documents he wrote verbatim to depict them "straight from the horse's mouth," as they say. In some cases, I corrected obvious mistakes of grammar and spelling that are inevitable when morphing from one language to the next on a routine basis as Henry did, and I spelled out most of his abbreviated dates and locations for better reader clarity. The written timeline of his life included a tremendous amount of condensed verbiage because his travels and activities were so extensive, giving him much to jot down in a relatively short period of time.

Discrepancies do exist between what was said in both sworn testimony and the earliest news articles from the trial and what some of the Wells descendants believe to be the case. My job isn't to play a mediator and determine which source of information is more accurate but to provide as many details as feasible from the earliest possible sources. I also ran into a number of inconsistencies between original news articles from 1882 and 1883 and those of more recent times. This is to be expected when retelling history, especially sordid history to which each raconteur likes to add his own oomph. Details tend to change with every passing generation. With that in mind, the information I chose to provide here is primarily from the original sources to ensure that the facts I relate have not been contaminated by time.

So here it is, the most comprehensive piece ever written about Henry Debosnys. With other deadlines looming, I relinquish all that I've ever collected regarding this case to you, my able audience, and trust that someone out there will determine who Henry was and finally crack the code that has eluded so many (including myself) for so long.

CRUEL WHEEL OF FATE

ACCIDENT AT THE MINES.—*Whallonsburgh, Dec. 12, 1870.*—*On last Saturday morning, Dec. 10ᵗʰ, about ten o'clock, a man by the name of John Wells, a resident of this town, was killed in Split Rock Ore Bed, situated a few miles south from Split Rock. It appears that there was a large piece of stone and ore in the roof of the mine that was loose, and the men employed tried to get it down but failed. About ten o'clock on Saturday, after firing a blast, it came down. It happened that there were three men standing near the loose piece in the roof, John Wells being about under the rock when it came down, striking him on the head, cutting the skull through and letting out the brains, also breaking one of his legs in two pieces, and cutting the other almost off. He was taken home in a wagon, as he lived about three miles or more from the mine. Those that were near him say he never took a breath after the piece struck him. The weight of the piece was about eight hundred. He leaves a wife and three children to mourn his loss. He was a hard working and an honest man. By his hard labor he bought a small piece of land on or near the lake, and had built him a house and was doing well.*
—Plattsburgh Sentinel, *Friday, December 16, 1870*

And so it was that in one earth-shattering instant at Split Rock near Lake Champlain, John Wells—beloved young husband and father—met his doom at thirty-three years of age, unintentionally setting the cruel wheel of fate in motion for his grieving, pregnant widow. Twelve years down the road, while passing through that same unfortunate vicinity on Split Rock Mountain, an unspeakable horror awaited Elizabeth "Betsey"

Wells. But with a baby on the way and three young daughters to support by herself, the thirty-year-old's immediate concern was simply to keep food on the table and a roof over her family's heads—and that she did well, perhaps too well, if one of the theories regarding a motive for her eventual demise is to be believed.

In 1840, Betsey was born Elizabeth Reed to Thomas Reed and Kate Casey of Ireland. When her mother died, her father moved the family to America, the "Land of Opportunity," settling in beautiful Essex County, the most mountainous county in the state of New York. In 1863, Betsey married Essex County native John Wells, a mining engineer from Chesterfield who worked at the Split Rock Iron Ore Bed. The couple's seven happy years together at their Whallon's Bay farm near Lake Champlain produced four daughters: Rebecca Jane, Mary Ellen, Eliza and Phoebe. The latter never knew her father, as John's life was cut short when she was yet in utero. A Wells descendant said in the 1970s that daughter Eliza's name was actually Louisa; however, since the girl was sworn in as Eliza at the murder trial in 1883, her name appears as such in news articles covering the trial. Following the accident that claimed John Wells's life—but due to the fact that the ore bed wasn't proving as profitable as others in the area—the company at Split Rock soon closed and never reopened. However, a financial settlement to Betsey Wells for her husband's accidental death was reached years later and allegedly publicized in the Burlington newspaper (across Lake Champlain), though I've been unable to locate that particular article. Betsey reportedly secreted about $300 away (now equivalent to $6,000) in a compartment that John Wells had built under the windowsill where she could access it on an as-needed basis for food and other essentials. After ten long, difficult years of hard work and selflessness, things must have finally seemed to be looking up for the industrious widow. Her daughters had grown into fine young ladies, ten to eighteen years old, and her property had grown to fifteen acres of prime real estate. But the lonely decade of toil had taken a toll on the widow's spirit, as it would on anyone's. So when Betsey's daughters brought home a charismatic stranger named Henry one fateful day, she must surely have welcomed the male company and adult conversation long missing from her dinner table. It was later speculated that the newcomer's chance encounter with Betsey's daughters was a ploy to gain access to the wealthy widow he had heard so much about.

Henry Deletnack Debosnys arrived in the village of Essex on May 1, 1882, and wasted no time in pursuing Ms. Wells—even though he himself was a widower of fewer than two months. We can only presume that he spared

Betsey that minor detail. With his incredible life story, the well-educated foreigner apparently turned on the charm and somehow won over his love interest. (After all, how many men in rural Northern New York can say, "I love you," in six different languages?) He was a real gentleman, a Parisian, he told her. By the time he confessed that he was presently down on his luck, it was too late for the good-hearted widow. Wells to turn her back on him. Some sources say that she hired him as a farmhand, and their relationship quickly progressed from there. Five weeks after meeting the worldly stranger, on June 8, 1882, Mrs. John Wells became Mrs. Henry Debosnys, and that singular lapse in good judgment was her downfall—and ultimately his, as well.

Some of Betsey's descendants believed that she had married Henry a full year earlier than reported, but that would have been impossible. Public assistance records from the French Society in Pennsylvania, as well as sworn testimony by dozens both locally and out of state, confirm that he was married to Celestine Debosnys and living in Philadelphia until he moved to Essex on May 1, 1882. To give you an idea of how hushed the wedding was, even Betsey's own brother, John, who lived nearby, didn't believe that she was married when she arrived on his doorstep one day, introducing her new husband, whom John had never seen before. By all accounts, very few of the locals knew who Henry was before his name and likeness were plastered all over every North Country paper and beyond. The *Plattsburgh Sentinel* of August 4, 1882, was the voice of the majority when it said that Betsey was "the well-known widow lady of that neighborhood who, but a few weeks previous, had married a comparative stranger named DeBosney." (The marriage actually occurred about eight weeks before the murder, not "a few weeks previous.")

Betsey's daughters would later recall in court that from the moment the two became husband and wife, Henry had begged Betsey to turn the deed for the property over to him. The new bride must have known from day one that she had been duped. Sensing his misguided intentions, Betsey steadfastly refused to accommodate the request. And she steadfastly refused to disclose to him where she hid the settlement money he knew she had. Her refusal to comply was an immediate and constant source of contention in the household. The couple fought bitterly, as Betsey became increasingly determined to prevent Henry from getting his hands on her property or wealth. It would be saved for her daughters in the event of her own death, not for a new husband whose real motives for marrying her were becoming increasingly, startlingly transparent. Betsey must have realized that she had given her heart too easily, allowing herself to be conned by this man and tricked into a loveless marriage just for her money. Thus, Henry realized that his plan to march right into Betsey's life and help himself to her wealth was futile; but instead of just leaving her and moving on to the next unsuspecting victim, he came up with a new plan. It was a cold and calculated course of action that would send shock waves rippling through the community—a course of action Betsey Wells never saw coming.

"She Perished Young"

She died like golden insect in the dew
Calm and pure; and not a chord was wrung
In her deep heart, but love, she perished young
But perished wasted by some fatal flame
That fed upon her vital, and there came
Death sweeping lightly, like a stream
Along her brain, she perished like a dream!
                    —*husband H. Debosnys, Elizabethtown,*
          Essex County, New York, December 12, 1882

On Monday, July 31, 1882, Henry asked Betsey to go with him on an outing to Port Henry. In his first statement to the press on August 4, 1882, just days after that fateful trip, he told the *Plattsburgh Sentinel*, "I wanted my wife to go with me and hire a farm of thirty-four acres near Mineville and leave the Essex farm for her daughters. Monday we drove to Port Henry to see the farm and stayed there overnight." But he told Betsey's daughter, sixteen-year-old Eliza, according to her sworn testimony the following year, that his father had arrived in Port Henry from France a couple of days earlier and wanted to meet Betsey and give the couple some furniture, a piano and a horse. He added that Betsey might stay "and clean house" if they could convince his father to buy a "nice brick house" there. Eliza later recalled her mother's reservations about leaving, especially since she was not feeling well that day, but she quietly confided to Eliza that "she would go and see what he had got." After all, he was her husband now, for better or for worse.

In 1973, Betsey's great-grandson told Billie Allen of the *Mountain Laurel* that the information regarding the purpose of the trip to Port Henry in articles written in 1882 was inaccurate. His grandmother, Rebecca, told him that Henry and Betsey were going to a fair that day, which contradicts what Eliza told the jury in 1883. Regardless of the purpose of that outing, it would be Betsey's last trip—and, for that matter, Henry's. The events that transpired after the couple left their home that Monday were pieced together following a thorough investigation, questioning of dozens of witnesses by authorities and reporters and a sensational, well-publicized trial.

According to Eliza Wells, Henry, whom she never trusted or respected, was in a hurry to leave that day, demanding that she bring him the horse and growing impatient when she refused on account of "a sore finger." When the child asked where they were going, her stepfather was quiet for a moment (perhaps needing time to get his story straight). After blabbering something about meeting his father in Port Henry and perhaps leaving Betsey there to clean the brick house for the old man, the two were off. That was the last time Eliza saw her mother alive. When the couple arrived at the Sprague Hotel in Port Henry, Betsey went inside while Henry weaseled his way out of paying to put up their horse for the night at Northrup's Stable by telling William Northrup that Betsey was inside with the money. The next morning, when he returned to retrieve the horse, he lied again, saying that he had left the money with the hotel clerk and adding that he was in a hurry to go and meet his father, who had just arrived with a "fine team [of horses] from Cohoes." Needless to say, Northrup never got paid.

One can only imagine what was going through Betsey's head at this point in the trip. Surely, she must have realized that Henry's father was not in Port Henry after all. And she must have wondered—perhaps out loud—what was going on. Or maybe Henry really had shown her a house, and she rejected the idea outright, refusing to leave her young daughters in Essex (and infuriating him before their return trip). We'll never know. Nevertheless, witnesses saw them at a store in Westport on Tuesday, August 1, where they picked up some food for a picnic lunch and proceeded north onto Lake Road, heading back the same way they had come. The previous day, they had been seen traveling in a southerly direction past the Bill Blinn, Allen Talbot, Edmund Floyd and Harry Allen farms on Split Rock Mountain. Henry had been wearing a crisp white shirt, and Betsey was decked out in a dark bonnet and a black dress, according to Blinn. This information became an important issue during trial. Eliza explained that normally her mother wore a hat, not a bonnet, but she wore the bonnet on that particular

To MY poor wife

Elizabeth "Betsey" Wells beside her grave. Drawing by Debosnys, December 18, 1882.
Courtesy of the Collection of Brewster Memorial Library/Essex County Historical Society.

trip at Henry's behest, Eliza believed, because he didn't want her mother to be easily recognized. Betsey nodded politely, nevertheless, at Blinn as they passed by his homestead on Monday. On Tuesday, the couple was spotted again by Mr. Floyd and the Talbots, and Harry Allen said that he heard them arguing as they approached.

Allen Talbot was working on the Blinn farm that day when he realized that he needed a rake back at his house. It was about half past one o'clock in the afternoon. On his way, the horse suddenly "gave the alarm by snorting and acting in a strange manner," according to the Elizabethtown *Post & Gazette* of August 3, 1882. It had become agitated by something in the woods off the side of the road up ahead, so Talbot looked in the direction from which the horse was pulling away just in time to catch a glimpse of a figure he believed to be Henry Debosnys. The man was lurking in the underbrush holding something white in his hand, Talbot recalled, and he seemed to be attempting to creep out of the farmer's view. Talbot thought it was a bit peculiar, but then again, for all he knew, Henry was just looking for a place to relieve himself. Continuing on his way, he spotted the couple's horse and empty wagon along the side of the road and wondered where Betsey was. Something wasn't adding up.

By the time Talbot returned to the same spot after grabbing his hay rake, the couple's horse and wagon were gone, only to reappear moments later proceeding slowly up the road near the Blinn farm. Talbot speculated in court that Henry had mounted the horse and turned off onto an old, little-used side road just after he saw him lurking in the woods—otherwise, he would have passed him on his return to Blinn's. But instead of approaching Henry and asking if everything was okay, Talbot hid in the barn and watched him go by, noting that he had changed out of the white shirt he had been wearing moments before and was instead wearing a patterned shirt. Talbot then found Blinn and told him of Henry's suspicious behavior and of how the horse had become agitated at something it saw in the woods nearby.

The two men hurried down the road to see if anything was amiss. There they found wagon tracks leading to a piece of an old road, and there were signs of a recent struggle, including little droplets of fresh blood on the leaves. As the men followed the crimson-dotted trail, they came to a depression in the soil that looked as if someone had begun to dig a hole. Standing at the crime scene, they noticed cracker crumbs scattered about haphazardly and a flattened trail where something had recently been dragged through the brush. With a sinking feeling in their guts, they followed it to the trail's end. There, in a secluded spot some seventy feet off the quiet road, they found the body of their forty-two-year-old friend and neighbor, Betsey Wells, covered lightly with leaves and branches. Moving a small amount of debris from the victim's face confirmed their worst fears. Carried by adrenaline, the two gentlemen raced to the nearest telegraph station at Whallonsburg and sounded the alert to local officials that Betsey's new husband had just killed her.

THE ARREST

Meanwhile, back at the ranch, Henry (oblivious that he had just become the Adirondack's "most wanted") was allegedly ransacking the Wells homestead and prying up window casings in search of the deed and money Betsey had refused to give him. When he was unable to find either, he headed to the Bruce residence looking for Betsey's daughter Rebecca. Surely, she would know where her mother's important documents and riches were hidden. For a man who had presumably just murdered his own wife in cold blood, he didn't even break a sweat as he stood in the yard speaking to Mr. Bruce. Then Henry produced a letter from his father as proof that the patriarch was on his way to Port Henry to move into a house he had purchased there. For good measure, he added that Betsey was busy cleaning the house even as they spoke. He needn't have wasted his breath (or his time) on the tale. Rebecca, as it thankfully turned out, was working at the James Ross house in Essex that day and not at the Bruce residence. So that stop was of no use to Henry. Once again, he left empty-handed. Moments later, John Mather stopped by the Bruce residence and noticed a ten-dollar bill lying on the ground outside, right where Henry had been standing. He showed it to the Bruces, who told him that it must have fallen out of Henry's pocket when he reached in to grab his father's letter. Apparently, Henry had a few bucks on him after all, contrary to what he told the guy at Northrup's Stable in Port Henry that morning. The question is: did he have it before or after the murder? My guess is not until after.

Unidentified female drawn by Debosnys while in jail. *Courtesy of the Collection of Brewster Memorial Library/Essex County Historical Society.*

Henry's next stop in search of Rebecca Wells was Soper's Mill (Boquet), where he instead bumped into Betsey's sister and told her the same thing he had told the Bruces. An early map I found that was roughly sketched by an unidentified witness to show Henry's wanderings of July 31 and August 1 (as best they could surmise) included his mother-in-law's house where, the drawing noted, "Debosny, after search [for jewels and money at the Wells cottage] went to mother-in-law in Whallonsburgh and tried to get money from her, then returned to Essex." But Betsey's mother, Kate, died overseas before Betsey's father moved the family to Essex County, so I'm not sure to whose mother-in-law that notation referred (unless they meant his stepmother-in-law, if her father had remarried and lived in Whallonsburgh). Nor am I sure how accurate the rest of the map of Henry's purported activity was. At any rate, he then proceeded to the post office to request that his wife's mail be forwarded to Port Henry, probably to make the story he'd been telling everyone appear more convincing. It was a move that he would immediately regret.

Just as he arrived, the assistant postmaster, Wesley Hoskins, received the message from Talbott and Blinn on the telegraph machine behind the counter stating that Henry had just killed Betsey. The map reads, "The telegraph operator received message while Debosny was standing in post office. As constable, he arrested Debosny." But news articles relaying the testimony from the trial said that Hoskins handed the note discreetly to George Tucker to take to the deputy constable, Bill Mulvey. Hoskins then kept Henry engaged in casual conversation as a stalling tactic until the constable arrived. Thankfully, that happened quickly. Mulvey strode into the post office just as Henry was heading out and handcuffed him right there in the doorway.

Hoskins's brother, Charles, held the accused man still and John Townshend frisked him. The Whallonsburg correspondent for the *Post & Gazette* said that Henry "seemed to make no effort to get away, as he committed the deed in a lonely place and on a road traveled but little." In other words, Henry chose that particular location so nobody would notice him or find the body too quickly. That same August 3 article, the first one written about the murder, said that it "seems to have been committed with great deliberation, in an unfrequented locality; the body was carefully covered with leaves."

A few reports and later testimony stated that a pistol that had been recently discharged was found on Henry in the post office, but more sources, including the very first article published regarding the case, stated that there was no evidence found on the arrested man at all—no blood, no stained clothing and no weapons. His wagon outside the post office, on the other hand, was loaded with evidence that didn't bode well for Henry, regardless of how it got there or by whom. There were three pistols, including one with two empty chambers, some cash, a bloodied knife, two bloodied rings that had belonged to Betsey and her purse (although Eliza admitted that she had never seen that particular purse of her mother's before). News articles didn't say where these items were situated in the wagon—whether they were tucked away where nobody could see them or lying right out in the open. If Henry's explanation—implausible as it was—was to be even remotely considered, the items like the knife and rings would have to have been well hidden even from Henry's view. With the accused still insisting that his wife couldn't possibly be dead and that she was alive and well in Port Henry, Hoskins promptly humored the man by acting as if he was about to send a telegram to the Sprague Hotel. But when Henry changed course and told Hoskins that, on second thought, perhaps Betsey was at her brother's house in Mineville, he was quickly led away. The constable, according to the *Plattsburgh Telegram* of August 3, 1882, had quite the time delivering Henry to the jail in Elizabethtown that evening:

> *A scene of wild excitement ensued, and it was with difficulty that the prisoner was conveyed amid threats of violence along the way, to the county jail in Elizabethtown. He is an utter stranger in that region, unknown to anybody; to Mrs. Wells, he had been married only a few weeks.*

If Henry's plan had been to flee the area by catching the ferry from Essex to Burlington, Vermont, as some believed was his intention, it was foiled the moment he paused long enough to continue his futile charade at the post office. The victim was an honorable woman; the witnesses were honorable locals; and Henry, the accused, was a complete and utter stranger from a foreign land. Enough said. The *Plattsburgh Sentinel* announced that the "circumstantial evidence of DeBosny's guilt seems conclusive." Circumstantial evidence? *Seems* conclusive? Back then a man's fate could be determined in less than ten minutes of contemplation based entirely on circumstantial evidence.

In the midst of the chaos at the post office, Dr. Atkins of Essex was dispatched to the dreadful scene of the crime, with Blinn and Talbot leading the way. There, Betsey Wells's body was surrounded by a number of local men who had volunteered to guard it until the doctor arrived. She was lying supine in the wooded hollow with two "pistol wounds" to the head and cheek, neither of which had been lethal. She had been shot in the cheek below the left eye and on the crown of her head. Although the latter shot failed to penetrate her skull, it was believed that it had rendered her unconscious before her throat was sliced clear to the bone. News articles reported that a "great gash had been made in the victim's neck, severing the carotid artery and penetrating to the spine." When Atkins finished his examination of the corpse, the men loaded it onto a wagon for the solemn task of delivering it to the victim's house and family, where it would be prepared for burial, as was customary in the day. One can only imagine the horror those poor, young girls had to endure upon seeing their mother's body returned to them broken and lifeless that awful evening. Drs. Atkins, Eaton and Hale, along with County Coroner Dr. Pease of Crown Point, held a formal inquest on Wednesday, August 4, at which time the cause of death was officially ruled a homicide. Henry was returned to Dr. Atkins for a "preliminary examination," a necessary formality that had been overlooked in the excitement of his arrest. He was then remanded to the jail in Elizabethtown to await grand jury action. A reporter who visited him during his first days in jail described the man whose name was suddenly known to all:

Debosnys is about five feet six inches tall, has black hair and a brown mustache, with high cheek bones. His eyes are a peculiar light brown, with an expression not calculated to impress one favorably. He has a high, well-developed forehead, which is disfigured on the left side by a scar two inches long, made, he says, by a rebel saber in 1862. His left wrist is tattooed on the back, with two tri-colored French flags with crossed staffs, and an anchor with a coiled cable. He has also the scar of a saber cut across the knuckles of his right hand.

While it was originally reported that the prisoner bore only the one tattoo on his wrist, after his passing his entire body was found to be covered with tattoos from his neck to his toes—a practice not uncommon in France at the time, especially among military personnel, convicts and those in secret societies. Although we would later learn that he likely fell into all three of those categories, initially he provided the authorities with only an abbreviated background of his life, along with his theory of how Betsey ended up dead:

> *I was born in Portugal forty-six years ago and was educated for the Catholic priesthood in Paris. I stayed at college two years and then left for America, as I decided to become an Episcopalian. I was then about seventeen years old. I came to Essex from Philadelphia four months ago and sailed my own yacht all the way. I came via New York, the Hudson River, and the Champlain canal and lake. I came to work at my trade—that of a painter. I married the deceased June 8. I am innocent of the crime charged against me.*
>
> *Over three weeks ago, a Scotchman, about sixty years old, with long gray whiskers came to my house and wanted something to eat. I gave it to him. He asked me if he could sleep in my barn. I allowed him to do so. He slept there three weeks, and I introduced him to my wife as my father. He got his meals at our house. I wanted my wife to go with me and hire a farm of thirty-four acres near Mineville and leave the Essex farm for her daughters. Monday we drove to Port Henry to see the farm and stayed there overnight. Tuesday we started to drive home, going by the old road. When about six miles from Essex, we met the old Scotchman, and he asked us if we had brought anything to drink. I answered that we had some whiskey, and we got out of the wagon and sat down in the woods. I got drunk and fell asleep. After sleeping some time, I was awakened by William Brown, the Scotchman, who asked me if I was not going home. I asked him where my wife was, and he said she had gone home long ago. I then started for home and did not know anything was wrong until I was arrested at Essex. I know nothing of the murder. I know I did wrong in introducing Brown to my wife as my father, but I never thought he intended to kill her.*

The Scotchman story was a doubtful tale that belied the intellect Henry would ultimately reveal. For one thing, if a man named Brown had been sleeping in their barn and eating at their table for the previous three weeks, and if Henry had introduced him to Betsey as his father as he claimed, then why had he told Betsey, her sister, the postmaster and the Wells girls that his father had "just arrived" in Port Henry from France and wished to meet his new wife? Did he have two fathers? Furthermore, Henry's real father was Portuguese, and his mother was French—of that, there's little doubt. Betsey's own father, Thomas Reed, was a true Scottish immigrant, but Henry's father? And if, as Henry claimed, Betsey had gone home from their roadside picnic while her husband was asleep in the woods, how did she go? On foot? They only had the one horse and wagon. Finally, if William Brown had really been wandering down the same quiet road at the same time that Henry and Betsey happened to be returning from their Port Henry trip, you can be sure that he would have been seen by Messrs. Floyd, Blinn and Allen and by Mrs. Talbot—the vigilant quartet who recalled every minuscule detail of their encounters with Betsey and Henry that day. Hence, the only believable part of "The Scotchman Did It" tale is the name Henry gave the Scotchman, Brown being the second most common Scottish surname.

EXTRA! EXTRA! READ ALL ABOUT IT

This crime was destined to be highlighted in the annals of Adirondack history. A well-respected woman, the victim of a brutal slaying that left four girls orphaned—and her new husband, a mysterious Frenchman she barely knew, the alleged killer. The sensational story would far outlive the ill-fated couple, thanks to publicity spanning two centuries. Besides the local media, particularly the Elizabethtown *Post & Gazette*, the *Plattsburgh Sentinel* and *Republican*, the *Essex County Republican* and the *Ticonderoga Sentinel*, the story captured the interest of the big leagues, like the *New York Times*. The *Times* ran several stories on the case. Its first article (below), from August 6, 1882, would leave the reader begging for more information. The saga proved to become so sensational over the next year that, by the time the *Times* ran its final story on the matter, the journalist conveyed a sense of disappointment that the story was over, like that felt when one turns the last page of a book he couldn't put down.

"A Wife's Fearful Death"
'Her Body Found in the Woods and Her Husband Accused of Killing Her'

Troy, N.Y., Aug. 5—Considerable excitement prevails in Essex County over the recent murder of a woman by her husband, Henry Deletnack De Bosnys, who is now in jail at Elizabethtown. The circumstances of the case are peculiar. About four months ago De Bosnys appeared in Essex village, having come there in a yacht. He was accompanied by a colored woman who passed as his wife. After remaining a short time, he sailed away, but returned on the following day, and stating that he had found employment for the woman in Burlington, Vt., left again, taking her with him. Subsequent events have given color to a rumor that De Bosnys drowned the woman in Lake Champlain. After an acquaintance of but four weeks, he was married to Mrs. Betsey A. Wells, a respectable widow of Essex, who, since her first husband's death, has provided for her four daughters. She owned a farm of 15 acres, and her marriage with De Bosnys was followed by frequent quarrels between them, caused by her refusal to assign her property to him. On Monday last De Bosnys and his wife drove to Port Henry, and it is supposed that while returning, they stopped by the roadside to eat lunch. They drove down an unfrequented road, and the wagon was seen later with De Bosnys as the only occupant. The suspicions of a farmer, who had noticed De Bosnys skulking in the woods, were aroused, and a search was made and the woman's dead body was found in a hollow, covered with leaves. Two pistol wounds were in the head, and there was a great gash in the neck, penetrating to the spine.

It is thought that De Bosnys and his wife had renewed their quarrel, and that he had killed her in a passion. He was arrested in Essex with two revolvers in his possession, one of 22-caliber, the size of the bullets found in the body, with two chambers recently discharged. De Bosnys states that he was born in Portugal, and is 46 years old. He says he was educated for a Catholic priest in Paris, and that he came to this country when 17 years of age. Four months ago, he left Philadelphia for Essex, in his own yacht, coming by way of New York, and thence up the Hudson River and the Champlain Canal. He says that three weeks ago a Scotchman came to his house hungry, and he gave him food, introducing him to Mrs. De Bosnys as his father. De Bosnys's statement continues: "On Monday my wife and I drove to Port Henry to inspect a farm I was endeavoring to induce my wife to purchase. On returning, and when six miles from home, we met the Scotchman, and we stopped and drank from a bottle of whisky. I got drunk and fell asleep in the woods. Awaking again, I asked the Scotchman where my wife was, and he said she had gone home. I started for home and knew nothing of the murder until arrested." His story is regarded as very improbable, and he is thought to be an escaped criminal who is concealing his identity. The prisoner has been attacked with epileptic fits in jail. He speaks six languages.

Latin

Non declines cor meum in verba malitiæ,
ad excusandas excusationes in peccatis.

Portuguess

Comoderondas inaxia beco olonda inoto para
Imbiabo Kotqronc molonk niarotan perana.

French

A quoi nous sert de faire envie, Le même Destin doit nous unir
A peine entrons nous dans la vie, que comme vous il faut mourir

English

You would not swear upon the bed of death.
Reflect; your Maker now could stop your Breath.

Spaniola

Cata tornalte vaxixui ydubulos menjis de la crina,

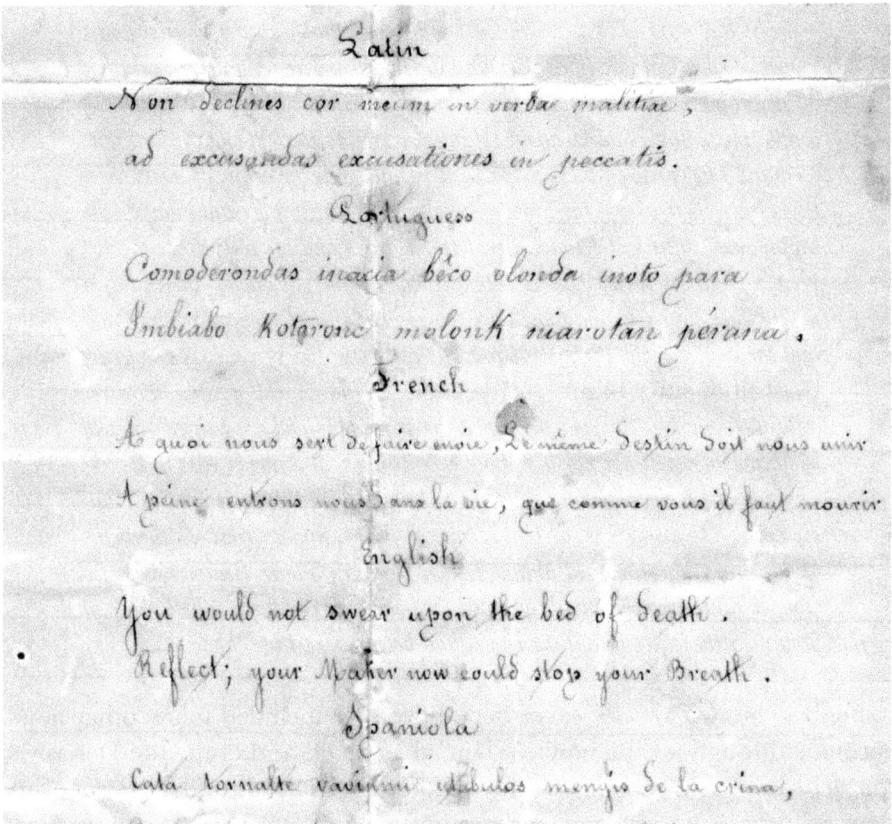

Sample of Debosnys's handwriting in five languages. Greek is missing. *Courtesy of the Collection of Brewster Memorial Library/Essex County Historical Society.*

So it wasn't just the dreadful crime that made the case so newsworthy. Right or wrong, it was the mystique of the criminal. Starting in August 1882, every weekly newspaper in the area scrambled to run stories of the crime (and the criminal). In the early days following the murder, all of the local papers were on the same page, so to speak, regarding the case. The same information was repeated in various forms, like the following article published by the *Plattsburgh Sentinel* on August 11, 1882:

> *On the eighth of June last, less than eight weeks before the murder, DeBosnys was married to a respected widow named Betsey A. Wells, who, by her own industry, had provided for her four daughters, and also accumulated some property since her first husband's death. Mrs. Wells owned a farm of fifteen*

acres in the town of Essex, and it is supposed that a desire to secure this property led to both the marriage and the murder. The union occurred after an acquaintance of but four weeks, and the frequent quarrels between the couple must have caused hasty repentance on the part of the unfortunate woman. The cause of these disputes, it is said, was the desire of DeBosnys to get his wife to assign her property to him…In this unpleasant manner, the couple lived until last Monday, when DeBosnys and his wife drove to Port Henry. While returning, it is supposed the couple got out of their wagon to eat their lunch in the woods by the roadside, that they quarreled, and that the woman was then murdered… [After the body was discovered by Talbot and Blinn,] *officers were on the track of the murderer within two hours after he committed the crime. He fled west three miles to Whallonsburg, thence north to Boquet five miles, and thence east to Essex, covering about eleven miles by his devious way, when the direct road was but six miles. On his arrival at Essex, he was placed under arrest, as the news of his crime had preceded him…Joseph Benway, James Benway, Charles Cooper, and Orrin Reynolds guarded the body* [of Betsey], *which had not been disturbed except that the leaves had been moved from the face.*

Besides the two articles excerpted above, I've included many other news accounts throughout the book. When all was said and done, the Debosnys murder case would become the most widely covered Adirondack event of its time, with press coverage extending throughout New York State and New York City, into Canada, Massachusetts and Vermont and all the way overseas to Paris. News coverage in the North Country began with an article in the local paper two days after the murder that was simply called "Murder." But the titles grew progressively longer, louder and more descriptive until the climactic day Henry was hanged, when headlines screamed, "EXECUTED! Henry Delectnack Debosnys (So Called) Pays the Penalty for Murder."

"JENKINS HOTEL"

Sheriff Talbot...has a crafty prisoner in this educated French murderer.
—Malone Palladium, *November 23, 1882*

Two days after Henry arrived at the jailhouse in Elizabethtown, he had an apparent epileptic seizure in his cell. Undersheriff Barber found the newly incarcerated prisoner lying in bed, muscles rigid and skin clammy, and he was bleeding profusely from a gash on his head acquired during the fit. He was given a shot of morphine by Dr. L.J. Daly, which seemed to bring some relief. He said he recalled having about ten such fits in the past fourteen years or so. Perhaps the stress of the predicament he found himself in aggravated the condition, for it wasn't long before he had another seizure in his cell. Dr. Bailey of Elizabethtown confirmed Dr. Daly's diagnosis of epilepsy and prescribed a mercury concoction for the symptoms. At the time, it was a common treatment for a number of ailments, but today we know that ingesting mercury in such amounts can cause severe, transient side effects—drooling, clumsiness, distorted vision and confused speech, difficulty walking and sleeping, poor concentration, hallucinations and loss of memory—everything you *don't* want your client to exhibit either before or during a trial as serious as one on which his life depends. The kicker is that mercury poisoning is linked to muscle tremors and violent spasms—precisely what Henry's physician was hoping to halt by providing the prisoner with "medicine."

One month after Henry settled into his new surroundings in jail (at what he called the "Jenkins Hotel" for Essex County sheriff Rollin L. Jenkins), the *Plattsburgh Sentinel* of September 15, 1882, reported, "The Essex County wife murderer will be tried at the Oyer and Terminer [a hearing and determination] to be held by Judge Landon at Elizabethtown the second Monday of December. Debosnys has made no preparations for his defense." But it was not for lack of trying. A month earlier, the same paper read: "Debosnys, murderer of his wife, has written from the jail at Elizabethtown, to M. Roustan, French consul at New York, asking $200 with which to procure counsel for his defense." He must have failed in his efforts, because former district attorney A.K. Dudley was ultimately appointed as his counsel.

Two months after his arrival in jail, Henry and inmate John Copeland—a convicted wife beater—discussed one morning, in hushed French, their plans to escape by attacking Undersheriff Barber when he arrived to let them out in the yard for their daily exercise. Another prisoner who understood some French overheard the conversation but didn't narc until after the plan had fallen through. Barber had arrived with a visitor instead of alone as usual. In so doing, he saved his own hide by squelching the prisoners' plan. The same informant told authorities that he had heard Henry telling Copeland details regarding Betsey's murder. Whether the informant was telling the truth or attempting to seek favor with the undersheriff was never documented. The important thing is that Henry's long, self-proclaimed winning streak of escaping prosecution for various infractions, great and small, had come to a grinding halt the day he arrived in Essex County.

By November—after three months' incarceration—Henry was clearly going stir crazy, which didn't help his cause, and his suspicious behavior prompted the sheriff to have him watched more closely. The *Malone Palladium* of November 23, 1882, described an unstable atmosphere at the old jailhouse, courtesy of Henry:

> *Sheriff Talbot, to whom the* Times *is indebted for some of the above statements, which were verified in an interview with DeBosnys, has a crafty prisoner in this educated French murderer. Although claiming to be friendless, DeBosnys has friends, and they have visited the outside of the jail a number of times during the night. On one occasion, Sheriff Talbot heard a noise about 10 o'clock at night. He took his revolver and went out, but the darkness was so thick he could see nothing. He heard footsteps, and from the sound says that two men were rapidly retreating toward the village. In the morning one of the prisoners, who was committed for a trivial*

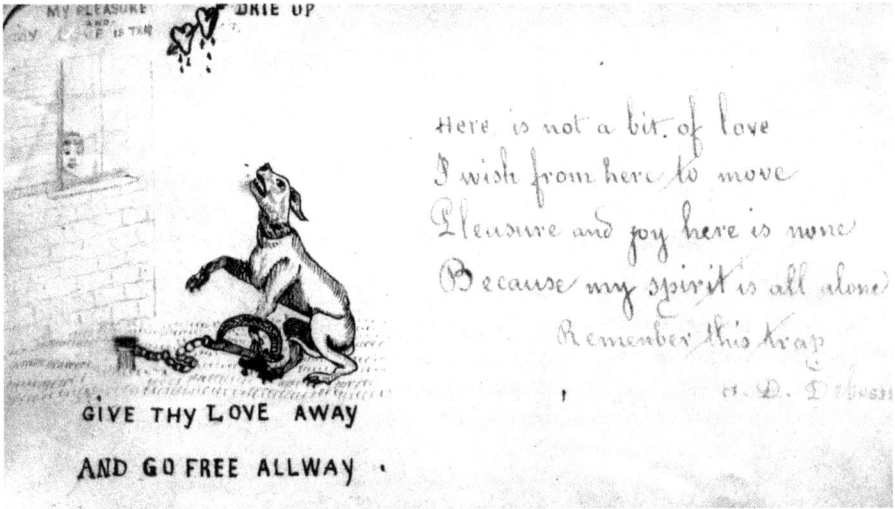

Henry's predicament. Drawn in the jailhouse Autographs book. *Courtesy of the Collection of Brewster Memorial Library/Essex County Historical Society.*

offense, informed the sheriff that two men had visited the jail the night before, equipped with a dark lantern, a rope and other articles, and had talked with DeBosnys. At another time, DeBosnys asked Sheriff Talbot in a sneering tone if he was to be hanged. That morning the prisoner was in a triumphant mood, and was so exultant that he aroused suspicion. A search revealed a piece of rope in his coat sleeve. A case knife taken to his cell that morning with breakfast was missing, and in its place an extra fork was found in DeBosnys's cell. He said that two forks were sent in with his breakfast, and no knife. Search revealed the missing knife secreted in DeBosnys's mattress. He is so troublesome that a close watch is kept on him continually, and a watchman is kept outside the prison every night.

On Monday, December 11, 1882, Henry pleaded not guilty at his oyer and terminer. The next night, he wrote the following in the jail's "Autographs" book in which he often scribbled or doodled when bored: "There stands a sentinel who spies our every action, hour by hour. By a Friendless man of Essex Co., N.Y., Henry Debosnys." The *Ticonderoga Sentinel* of December 22, 1882, reported, "DeBosney…will be tried at a special term to be held on the first Tuesday in March. A.K. Dudley of Elizabethtown was assigned as council, and it is safe to say that DeBosney will be ably defended. DeBosney says that he needs time that he may find the man who killed his wife."

During his nine-month incarceration, it became apparent that this was no run-of-the-mill, cold-blooded wife killer. He admitted unashamedly from day one that the name he currently went by, Henry Deletnack Debosnys, was an alias, which begged the question of why. From what was he was running? He later explained that, with a false identity, his family would be spared the details of his alleged crime and impending punishment. They would never learn of his shameful demise. And keeping the family name secret would also protect his father, sister and children (from what, he didn't say). But he came into Essex County with that alias, well before he ever met Betsey; the French Society in Pennsylvania had him listed under Debosnys, as well. So he had to have been dissociating himself from his real name prior to arriving in the North Country or even in Pennsylvania, for that matter. At any rate, true to his word, he did take his identity to the grave, leaving it up to us to figure out.

With Henry in custody, there was never a dull moment at the Essex County Jailhouse. Besides the steady stream of misguided visitors who were either sympathetic (believing the man was innocent) or just plain curious, there was some strange activity going on within his cell. Henry arranged somehow to have three trunks delivered to the jail from an unknown source. Two contained guns, knives and powder horns, according to a man named Henry Lawrence. Obviously, those items were quickly confiscated and never reached the inmate in his jail cell. But the third was a small, flat-topped trunk filled with personal documents, presumably including some of the biographical sketches, cryptograms, poetry and drawings he had created during his many journeys. During his incarceration, he would add to this collection of inked oddities—most of which would never be seen by the public for some seventy-five years. If he wasn't an enigma at the time, he would certainly become one when these insightful documents ultimately resurfaced.

Henry knew he was a dead man before the trial ever commenced. He spent hours in his cell sketching scenes of cemeteries and writing poetry about death and (rather surprisingly) heaven. He never spoke of hell, though one would have assumed it might have been of concern to him, considering his early aspirations to the priesthood. But, no, he was quite sure that he would go to heaven, where his three wives (that we know of) would await him with open arms, having both forgiven and forgotten his awful deeds. He was just as certain that those who condemned him to die would regret their actions and realize their folly too late. Much like Edgar Allan Poe (and others of the Dark Romanticism movement of the time),

Henry's poetry dealt primarily with death, mourning and the afterlife. But while both Henry and Poe had good reason to obsess over death, only Henry had both dealt it and was painfully aware that it was about to be dealt to him.

Not everyone back then appreciated the opportunity to read and interpret the alleged killer's poetry. The *Troy Times*, for example, noted brusquely on November 23, 1882:

> *The prisoner spends his time writing verses, or what he thinks is poetry, and he has over a ream of foolscap paper closely written. Much of this doggerel is written in Latin, French, and an unknown cipher, which Debosnys says is used in Europe quite extensively.*

If the cipher, or cryptography, was extensively used in Europe in the late nineteenth century, as Debosnys said, that could be an important tip—especially today when we can view images of most known ciphers throughout history right online. Henry's ciphers—or cryptograms, if you will—are discussed in greater length later in this book. But first, the notorious poems.

"DRAIRY IS THE THOUGHT OF DYING"

The following poems written by Henry illustrate what was going through his mind in regard to his impending demise. Considering the verbiage, there's a good chance they hold a number of clues to his identity.

One of many death-themed depictions drawn by Henry to illustrate his poems. *Courtesy of the Collection of Brewster Memorial Library/Essex County Historical Society.*

Strangers! who pass near this grave,
Let awhile your studious eyes engage in your head,
And when returning to your home, you may say,
We have seen the last home, where we have to go and stay.
From which is no return no more, no, no more—
And never feel the splendor of the sun, no more.
They turned their head, and as he spoke,
A sudden splendor all around them broke
And they beheld an orb, ample and bright.
Rise from the holy well, and cast its light
Round the rich city of the death, and the plain—
Shane out to bless the breaking of the chain
That now sink beneath an unexpected arm
And in a death-groom, give its last alarm.
Its hand full of joy, proclaim through Heaven
The triumph of its own soul forgiven
Joy, joy, here forever, my task is done
The gates of misery are passed, and Heaven is won.
The scene which I have journeyed over—
Return no more—no! no! no more.
This awakes my hourly sighing
Drairy is the thought of dying.
Let me resign a wretched breath
Since now that remain on me.
No other calm than kindly death,
To soothe my last trouble, my last misery.
But having sworn upon the holy grave
To conquer or perish, once more gave
Nor less in number, and we let them all stay:
Come with me now, I will give my life away
Yes, poor wretched—thine is such a grief,
Beyond all hope, all terror, all relief;
And dark, cold calm, which nothing now can break,
Or warm, or brighten, like the water on the lake.
Liberty now for me would be of a short season,
After my terrible suffering in this poor prison.
Though in my earliest life bereft
Lost in that sweet dream, such a change in life
Though hope deceived, pleasure left—

I wish to sigh my latest breath—
And go meet my poor wife into death.
To you all, my soul's affections move
My life had burned here like a stove
If your sorrow faith be over. I will try
To bless you, and your names, and go to die?

—*September 18, 1882 (Essex County Jail)*

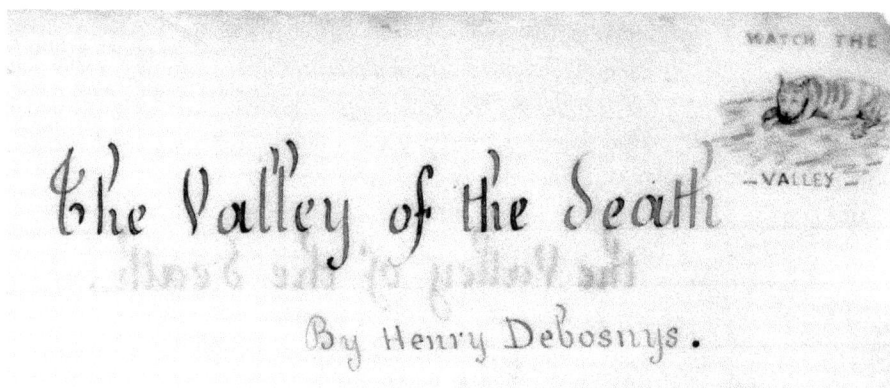

Created by Henry Debosnys in jail. *Courtesy of the Collection of Brewster Memorial Library/Essex County Historical Society.*

From the prison without freedom! oh who would not fly
For an eternity of freedom! oh who would not die.
In death's kindly bosom my last hope remain
The dead fear not chains, nor tyrants, the grave has no chains!
And oh! even if freedom from this world be driven,
I despair not, at least I shall find her in Heaven.
Rest dear bosom! no more sorrow shall pain thee,
Beam, bright eyelid! no more weeping shall stain thee,
What softened remembrance come over the heart,
In gazing on those, that we have been lost so long!
The sorrows, the joys, of which once they were part.

Still round them like visions of yesterday throng
As letters some hand hath invisibly traced,
When held to the flame, will steal out on the sight.
So many a feeling that long seemed effaced,
The warmth of a meeting like this make amends
For all the long years I have been wandering away?
To see thus around me my youth early friends,
As smiling and kind, as in that happy day!
So many a feeling that long seemed effaced from sight
The remembrance of a meeting like this bring to light.
Shall I ask the only friend who fights by my side
In the cause of today, if our creeds agree?
Shall I give up the friend I have valued and tried,
No, no, never, I like to see everyone free—
The thread of our life would be dark, heaven knows—
If it were not with friendship and love intertwined.
And I care not how soon I sink to repose
When I know all my friends are dear to my mind.
It was that friend, the beloved of my bosom that was near,
And who made every scene of enchantment more dear
Who felt how the best charms of nature improve
When we see them reflected from the look that we love.
Sweet Valley of the deaths! how calm could I rest—
In thy bosom of shade, with the friend I love the best,
Where the storms that I feel in this world should cease
And our hearts, like thy waters, be mingled in peace.
There is not in the wide world a valley so sweet
As that valley in whose bosom the bright waters meet.
Oh! the last ray of feeling and life must depart
Ere the bloom of that valley shall fade from my heart.

—August 29, 1882

the solitary grave
. or the hermit dying alone .

Created by Henry Debosnys in jail. *Courtesy of the Collection of Brewster Memorial Library/Essex County Historical Society.*

Like the hermit—he take a solitary grave
Below the pine trees, and he sang a stave,
Or two, or three, of some old requiem
As in their narrow home he buried them
And many a day before that blessed spot
He sate, in lone and melancholy thought,
Thinking upon the grave; and one had guessed
Of some dark secret shadowing his breast.
And yet, to see him, with his first gray hair
Floating alone in the valley-borne air,
And features chastened in the tears of woe,
In short, it was merely sad to see him so!
As a wreck of nature floating far and fast,
Upon the stream of time, to sink at last!
To his own heart that lonely hermit man
A tale of other days when passion ran
Along his pulses like a troubled stream
And glory was a splendor and a dream!
Of the fierce sunbeams fell upon its face,
And of his young life have—but the trace
Of some old thought came burning to the brain
Of the poor hermit, and he shrunk in pain
Too deadly to be shadowed or forgiven
To do such mockery in the sight of Heaven.

Poem and illustration by Debosnys on foolscap. *Courtesy of the Collection of Brewster Memorial Library/Essex County Historical Society.*

The image Henry sketched over the top of the following verse was in nearly too bad of condition to reproduce, but it depicted a lone tombstone with vines on either side bearing a red fruit. A goat in profile stands to the right of the tombstone, which reads: "To Henry D. Debosnys—Colonel of the 2^d Legions of Satory—International Society 1882."

My Own Grave

Ere is my grave, in all divine
And free from the old world it is
I will visit the Heaven with mine
Oh what a pride I wish to say this
My heart, soul, and senses are turned below,
Above me, in the moon-beam shone
With a pure light which from its hue
To my grave take me; for all I had, have gone.

—*Essex County, New York, August 10, 1882*

———◆———

Poor Henru—My Last Voyage and My Adieu

(Translated from French)

Before leaving you for this long journey
To you all my friends I bid adieu
I had only you, who gave me the courage
To bear so long my misery in this place
No regrets, my friends, to see me leave this world
For this dishonor, alas, on you will fall without pity
You will not be there the hour that I succumb
But your memory alone will remain to me in friendship
The people are so wicked that they would commit a crime
Rather than help me or deliver me from dishonor.
Their cry is only for my death or a land of exile
To satisfy the rage of the one I act happy
Bearing with patience the future of this judgment
Without every time making the promise of being there...
Our days are as variable as the weather
To promise a fair day and to take it when it comes
That is why, when of our life the terrible destiny

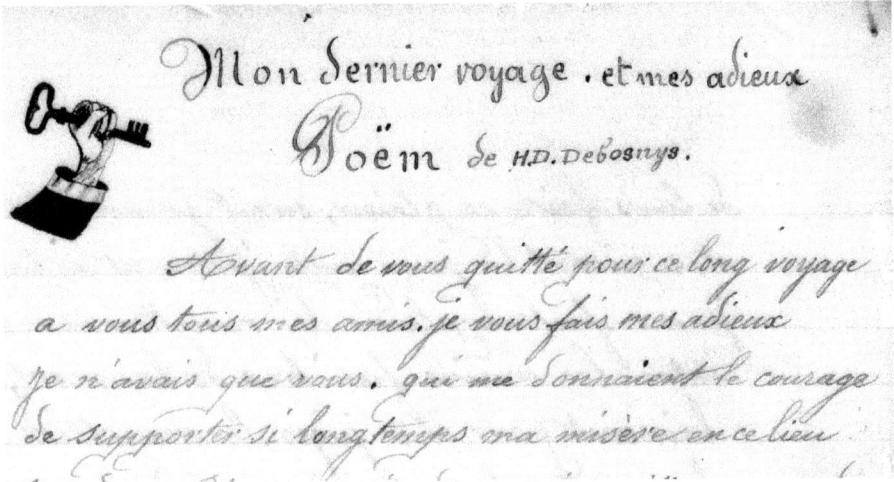

Another French poem by Debosnys. *Courtesy of the Collection of Brewster Memorial Library/Essex County Historical Society.*

Comes all at once—cut off the breath that animates us
Has shared the careless days of this world
To share without hope, of an intimate friend
The sweet moments which pass into the shadows
Like the smoke of the past carried away by the wind
As my enemies would like, I imagine
To see me go trembling like a child
Straight to the scaffold like a poor victim—
Of the lies of the poor wretched inhabitants
To give them this pleasure would be great folly
And supposing the joy that they feel in advance
I give myself the pleasure of laying aside my life
Into the funereal hands of death with confidence
Leaving for my judges the absent murderer.
Minute research will lead I hope
To the true guilty one who will take my place in the judgment
Since for a foreigner like myself they have no sympathy
For them as for you I would have died thus
Without thinking further people will say among themselves
That poor devil is dead, and we blamed him
We threatened him with pain of death without reason
It is our fault, but let's not think of it any more.
He was a foreigner.

They will not find on me if I leave this world
The last breath of my life flies away with our secrets
For my son whom I leave in this moment like a shadow
Of my life will not be initiated into the first degree
My death will be hidden from him as long as possible
To put far from him grief and despair
Who of a life so young will trouble the future
To bring back to him joy, happiness, and sweet liberty
To compare in society without being humiliated in it?

Rest in peace

The Eternal Judgment

(Translated from French)

Let us all assemble for this great feast
Where each of us breathes with so much courage
And perseverance, in case, yes, the trespass
Is to aid us to end this courageous work,
Of which God the Eternal is to give us the commandment.
Let our hearts and our souls follow his words
And no longer go astray in frivolous society,
Where like so many others they had fallen.
Our time is near and our minutes are numbered.
The hour of the great judgment is about to surprise us.
All, without exception, rich and poor,
At this holy tribunal will know the joys that await us.
We will all see one another again, though feeling our tears fall,
Which will fall gladly to water our pathway.
The heat of the day and the shadows will come to pass
But the word and the kingdom of God are holy.
O! God of Heaven, see my sobs and my tears,
Deign to hear the humble prayer of a poor prisoner.
Reunite now, those whom earth has taken by thy charm
For thou alone, alas, hast that power that I cease not to beg for.
On this earth where we groan awaiting the time—
Where the sound of the trump will announce to us thy judgment?

le cheval porte la dépêche.

Le jugement Eternel.

. il viens a grand pas le jugement de dieu.

Debosnys illustration. *Courtesy of the Collection of Brewster Memorial Library/Essex County Historical Society.*

The Abandonment

(Translated from French)

All on this earth, yes all abandon me
Just in the midst of my greatest torments.
But alas with the strength that God gives me,
Of men here below I fear not the chastisement,
My life here below, is it not to be compared
In this inconstant world, to the light of a candle
Which burns a moment if we are careful to watch over it
All at once melted it goes out, and the darkness finally falls.
In such deep shadows let our weary eyes
Half-close in the depths of sleep
Not to open again till morning.
My life, like that light of the candle
My last day and night until the approaching moment
When my judges, persecutors and false witnesses—so false
Who will pronounce the fatal sentence of my death
By strangling of the rope on the scaffold.
Innocent as my wife who was the victim, remorse
Does not pursue me in my sleep
The repose of my body, in the day as in the night

Was always calm, whatever in this prison I fashion.

The following is a poem Henry originally wrote for Betsey; he called it "To My Poor Wife" and illustrated it with a picture of her standing near her tombstone holding a bouquet of flowers. Later, when he rewrote the same poem and applied it to himself, he changed the title to "The Solitary Grave."

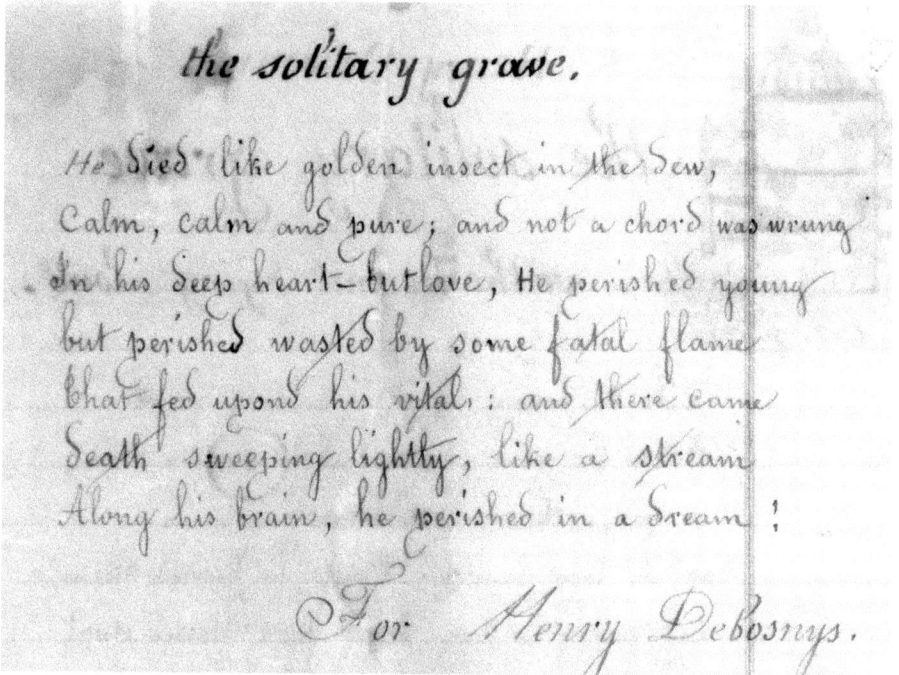

the solitary grave.

He died like golden insect in the dew,
Calm, calm and pure; and not a chord was wrung
In his deep heart—but love, He perished young
but perished wasted by some fatal flame
that fed upon his vitals: and there came
Death sweeping lightly, like a stream
Along his brain, he perished in a dream!

For Henry Debosnys.

Debosnys poem. *Courtesy of the Collection of Brewster Memorial Library/Essex County Historical Society.*

"A Murderer's Strange Story"

S ome have speculated that Henry Debosnys may have had something to do with the mysterious disappearance of Henry Lemaire, who vanished from his boardinghouse in Essex in the summer of 1873. Indeed, Debosnys and his wife Celestine *did* happen to be in Essex that summer for a brief stint from May through July while Debosnys worked as a painter. So there's a very good chance that he befriended the fellow Frenchman and was privy to information regarding his disappearance that was not previously considered at the time. (Coincidentally, the same quarry Lemaire had been employed at was suspended in 1872, following John Wells's terrible accident, putting Lemaire and others out of work. That may be when Henry Debosnys first learned of the Wells accident and the company's impending settlement with the victim's widow.) The fact that Henry chose to share his knowledge of the long-forgotten disappearance of Lemaire from his jail cell only served to add another twist to the increasingly bizarre tale that was his life. As reported in the *Malone Palladium* on November 23, 1882, the following is a portion of an article called "A Murderer's Strange Story." It is intended to provide you with insight into Debosnys's past, when he first lived in Essex; most people were unaware that he had lived there for a short time nine years before he returned to the area and married Betsey Wells.

> *Ten years ago last summer the village of Essex was agitated over the sudden and mysterious disappearance of Henry Lemaire, a Frenchman. He had been employed as a laborer in a stone quarry at Essex, and had accumulated*

about $500 by industry and thrift. He was unmarried and had no relatives or friends in the vicinity of Essex, and boarded with a fellow countryman. Work in the quarry which Lemaire had been employed was suspended in 1872, and he, with others, was thrown out of employment. He did not enjoy idleness, and quickly secured employment with a farmer named Tucker. He had followed this pursuit about two weeks, but had drawn no wages from his employer, and one evening quit work as usual, went to his boarding house, and there mysteriously disappeared.

Nothing has been heard of him. His sudden and unaccountable disappearance was made more mysterious by the fact that he took none of his personal effects with him. He left his trunk and clothing at his boarding house and an undrawn balance of wages due him was in the hands of the employer. His disappearance excited suspicion, was a nine days' wonder, and finally appeared to be forgotten. It recently has been recalled by the murder of Betsey DeBosnys whose husband is now in the Essex county jail, at Elizabethtown, charged with wife murder.

When DeBosnys was arrested for the murder of his wife, it was generally supposed that he went to Essex for the first time about four months before his arrest. This erroneous supposition the prisoner took no trouble to correct until a short time ago, when he began to tell of his previous residence in Essex. He several times dropped allusions calculated to excite curiosity in the mind of his jailer. Finally, he stated that he worked at his trade (a painter) in Essex ten years before, and mentioned several buildings he had painted. DeBosnys no doubt worked in Essex at the time he states, and he is, on reflection, well remembered by a number of residents. He remembers Lemaire and his disappearance, and gave a reporter the following account of what he claims to know.

DeBosnys formerly boarded at the same house with Lemaire, and occasionally heard conversation which excited his suspicion regarding the death of the latter. On one occasion he says the boarding-house keeper and his wife quarreled, and the husband struck his wife. The woman turned upon him and said he would get himself into trouble if he struck her again, and that she would give the murder away. This speech quickly quieted the irate husband, and after that time the woman was treated with marked consideration. DeBosnys noted this answer and its effect, and says that a short time afterward he asked the woman what had become of Lemaire. She turned pale and said she did not know; people said he was murdered, but if so, it happened so many days ago that it could never be found out.

> *He alleges that when Lemaire disappeared the boarding-house keeper had possession of his effects, and that three weeks afterward he broke open the missing man's trunk and took out the contents. The trunk contained letters and clothing, and the prisoner alleges that these letters are still in possession of the boarding-house keeper, but the clothes were all sold the day after his trunk was broken open to an Italian laborer on the railroad at Willsborough. DeBosnys says before the disappearance of Lemaire the boarding-house keeper was very poor, but a short time afterward, he purchased some property. DeBosnys made it his business before his arrest to investigate the matter, and intended to write to the prefect of police of Paris, and find out, if possible, where Lemaire's friends reside, so that they could come and ferret the mystery out.*
>
> *DeBosnys claims that in his investigations, he became convinced that Lemaire was murdered in his room, and that from what he has heard and seen, he believes that his body was interred under the boarding-house. What he bases this belief upon is something DeBosnys does not, and apparently can not, give a satisfactory reason for, but insists that investigation by the proper authorities will prove the truth of his allegations.*

What I wonder is whether Henry may have killed Lemaire and crafted the story above to gain favor with the authorities in charge of his incarceration by providing them with information to help solve an old mystery. After all, he didn't stay long in Essex after the man's disappearance. Former Essex County deputy sheriff William Davis and his wife researched and wrote a comprehensive report on Debosnys in 1961, after Davis went on a mission to find out all he could about the old case. While interviewing people for this paper, Davis was told that a man by the name of Joe Lehagaret was believed by some to be Debosnys's brother. He was also believed to have been involved in the disappearance and murder of Lemaire, though this was never proven. Davis was told that the case of the missing French "peddler" created much speculation, but the finger was pointed at Lehagaret—a "rough character" known to threaten his wife with a knife—when he came into some unexplained wealth shortly after Lemaire disappeared. Though he claimed the money had come from the settlement of a relative's estate in France, it still raised a red flag. Supposedly, several years after the unsolved mystery occurred, Lehagaret was helping some other men clear debris from a house that had been burned down when they uncovered some human bones. When one of the men pointed out lightheartedly to Lehagaret that it must be Lemaire's remains, Lehagaret paled and raced home.

For some reason, I've been unable to locate any articles pertaining to either Lemaire or Lehagaret in the newspaper archives, even though the article above stated that the disappearance of Lemaire created quite a stir in the community at the time. The Lemaire disappearance was largely forgotten after that incident, until Henry brought it up from his jail cell. But the fact that he brought it up at all makes me wonder if he had anything to do with Lemaire's disappearance and was trying to pass the buck under the guise of helping local authorities in exchange for more favorable treatment in jail. It also makes me wonder if Lehagaret really was Henry's brother, as well as the unidentified boardinghouse keeper of whom he spoke. Were Henry and Lehagaret both culpable in Lemaire's disappearance? And was Lehagaret also an assumed name, if he was, in fact, Henry's brother? Was their entire family on the run?

NINE-MINUTE VERDICT

Officers Durand, of Elizabethtown, and Reynolds, of Lewis, brought in the prisoner, Henry DeLetnack DeBosnys, and a more repulsive being we have never seen arraigned: small, weak, sickly, trembling, supported as he walked by the two officers, complexion sallow, countenance dejected, despondent, and whole demeanor cringing and cowardly. Seated with head drooped and eyes downcast, from his mouth issued a stream of saliva, the effects of mercury administered during his sickness of the past few weeks. We will not presume to analyze his motives or say how much of his helplessness and apparent, almost demented, condition was feigned.
—Plattsburgh Sentinel, *March 9, 1883*

I'll say one thing for the *Plattsburgh Sentinel*, it didn't mince words in March 1883 when it came to describing the foreigner arrested for killing one of the community's own. It didn't matter that Henry was being treated pharmaceutically with mercury and that each of the characteristics the reporter for that paper listed in his scathing description of the prisoner is a known symptom of mercury poisoning. Those present didn't realize the full scope of such poisoning at that time and believed that mercury could only have caused Henry's uncontrollable drooling and not any of the other symptoms he displayed. Today we know otherwise, of course, and we know that such symptoms are not feigned. But words in the mainstream media were not chosen as carefully in 1883 as they are today to reflect fair, impartial reporting. Instead, people's opinions about a criminal were based on the opinion of the reporter, regardless of the facts. Nevertheless—with or

Another Debosnys self-portrait, left in the jailhouse's Autographs book. *Courtesy of the Collection of Brewster Memorial Library/Essex County Historical Society.*

without their personal opinions—all of the local newspapers reported the trial comprehensively, providing the statements of each and every witness, in full-page accounts too long to reproduce in this book.

On March 6, 1883, Judge Landon presided over the courtroom in the Old Essex County Courthouse. Arod Dudley was Henry's defense attorney, along with his partner, Mr. Corbin; Rawland Kellogg was the prosecutor. Kellogg called Talbot, Blinn, Northrup, Mrs. Talbot and Rebecca Wells to the stand. The five witnesses testified and were cross-examined by the defense before being dismissed early, due to a severe snowstorm. On the second day, fourteen witnesses were called to the stand, including Eliza Wells; Messrs. Bruce, Mather, Lawrence, Hoskins, Barber, Chamberlain and Reed; and Drs. Atkins, Hale and Bailey. Henry took the stand, as well, such as he was. Although the mercury prescribed to him was taking a toll on his health and demeanor, causing him to slur his speech, he remained insistent that he had been so drunk in the woods on August 1 that he had no idea what had transpired while he was passed out. Several witnesses who denied that assertion were called to the stand during cross-examination. The Henry Debosnys they saw on the road that day at the time of the victim's demise seemed "perfectly sober," they all agreed (although many a drunk has appeared quite sober when he wakes from an alcohol-induced slumber).

The white shirt Henry had been seen wearing before the murder, as well as Betsey's dark veil and bonnet, were never recovered, leading the prosecutor to speculate that Henry had saturated the incriminating, blood-stained apparel with liquor and set it all afire. But wouldn't the smoke from a fire in the woods that afternoon have been seen by Blinn, the Talbots and the others who remembered every miniscule detail of the couple, right down to the white cloth in Henry's hands even at a distance? Smoke would have risen above the tree line and been quite obvious, wouldn't it? Furthermore, had the sight of smoke proved futile, wouldn't there at least have been evidence of a fire somewhere near the crime scene if Henry had, in fact, incinerated the apparel as suggested? There was not. This begs the question of how accurate the witnesses' testimony was in regard to the victim's and killer's clothing and whatever else they believed they saw. If smoke could not be seen rising above the tree line on a bright afternoon, then what else was missed? And what may have been reported inaccurately? Unfortunately for Henry, much of the testimony seemed to dwell on statements regarding the missing clothing that he and Betsey had allegedly been seen wearing before it disappeared off the face of the earth. I can understand a murderer trying to destroy damning evidence, like clothing he was wearing, that could tie him to the crime. But why burn the victim's bonnet and nothing else? What purpose would that have served? Was there ever a black bonnet—or a white shirt, for that matter?

Is it possible that Henry was telling at least a partial truth? Had some wayward Scotchman set him up? Had a stranger with a bone to pick encountered the couple that afternoon, waited for Henry to pass out, killed Betsey (to frame Henry), thrown the most damning evidence like the bloodied rings and single-bladed knife back into Henry's wagon to implicate him, tucked the missing apparel into a hobo bag and walked smugly off into the sunset, leaving a trail of false accusations directed at the wrong man behind him? Is it possible that when Talbot saw a man lurking in the underbrush, what he really was seeing was Henry awaking and searching for (but not finding) Betsey before he continued on his way home, confused and moving slowly? Not according to Henry's attorney, Corbin, who told the jury in his closing arguments that Henry had murdered his wife but had done it "rashly in a moment of excitement"; and since it was not premeditated, it was murder in the second degree. I can only wonder if Henry, lethargic under the heavy influence of mercurial poisoning at his trial, had his wits about him enough to comprehend what was being said to the jury on his behalf. It seems to me there were an awful lot of unanswered questions for a jury to determine a man's guilt beyond a shadow of a doubt. Nevertheless, the jury took only nine minutes to return its verdict: guilty of murder in the first degree. Henry broke down but agreed that there was no reason why the judge shouldn't set the sentence. So he was ordered returned to the jail until April 27, 1883—fifty-one days away—when he would be taken by the county sheriff and "hanged by the neck until dead," or, as one source claimed, "until dead, dead, dead."

"UNTIL DEAD, DEAD, DEAD"

The *Burlington Free Press* of April 17, 1883, reported, with an odd mixture of regret and empathy for the condemned, "Henry DeBosnys, one of the most extraordinary criminals of the age, is to be hanged April 27, at Elizabethtown, N.Y., a little village on Lake Champlain, directly opposite this city. His crime is commonplace enough, being that of wife murder, but his career has been a most remarkable one." It isn't so much the rare show of compassion toward Henry by the media that caught me off guard with that statement; it was the fact that there apparently was a time when murdering one's wife was considered "commonplace" by some!

Essex County deputy sheriff William F. Davis, in his comprehensive 1961 notes titled "The Debosnys Murder Case," said that the prisoner's demeanor changed overnight following his sentencing, according to various reports. The man who was once called a "poor, weak, sickly, cowardly, demented creature" in news accounts of the trial proceedings had suddenly become "a picture of physical and mental vigor and 'animal' courage" in the eyes of the media. Though he had rarely slept or eaten before the trial, from the first night following his sentencing, he had "slept and eaten soundly and heartily" and seemed suddenly "unconcerned at his approaching doom," according to the *Elizabethtown Post*. He continued to enjoy the company of sympathetic female visitors who brought him baked goods and treats, which provided him with a cheery respite from the grim task at hand (obsessively writing death-themed poetry). When he wasn't thinking up verses or sketching morbid scenes, he was busily writing his biography on legal foolscap. Eventually, he gave most of his creations to a woman who had shown him kindness that he wished to repay. But she never grasped the value of what she had received and kept the collection primarily to herself for the rest of her life (some thirty years). Perhaps she felt it was inappropriate to admit that she had accepted the unusual gifts from someone so loathed by so many, unlike Alonzo Petty, who was a young court officer in Elizabethtown in 1883. Petty told the *Ticonderoga Sentinel* fifty years later that he had "always cherished a paper given him by Debosny. On the paper is a poem written by Debosny and a pen drawing of a man, two women, and a church. He said that the church was a picture of a church near his boyhood home."

Chronicler that he was, Henry never turned down interviews with the local papers; they allowed him to talk about himself, and they were all too accommodating in sharing any tidbit he felt compelled to share, like the imaginary collection of animals he insisted were alive and well in his cell. Incarceration can do that to a man—and so can mercury poisoning, which is where the phrase "mad as a hatter" originated. (Mercury was once used in the production of top hats, and hatters who inhaled the fumes often went insane from the cumulative effects of mercurous nitrate on their nervous system.) Henry pretended to keep a baby who cried, a donkey that brayed, a dog that barked, a crow that cawed and so on. At least one reporter was impressed enough to pay him a compliment. George Brown of the *Elizabethtown Post* said that Henry was "a perfect mimic, and afternoons when he is locked in his cell, he opens his 'menagerie,' mimicking the several animals and birds very perfectly." Two weeks before his hanging, Henry requested that the *Post* visit him for an interview regarding his life. When the reporters arrived, they "found Debosnys sitting at a table, in the corridor of the lower floor in the new jail addition, busily engaged in writing…He was in good spirits and apparently perfect health. At his dictation, from a written copy before him, we wrote down [his life story]." Henry proceeded to read them the autobiography he penned in his jail cell, which is included in its entirety later in this book.

While some were busy calling on the governor of New York State to commute Henry's death sentence on grounds of insanity in the countdown to April 27, Henry had given up on waiting for a miracle. Instead, he was arranging the sale of his body, or his "body, flesh, bones, and blood," according to an article by M.B. Allen in the *Press Republican* on July 22, 1977. In return, Henry received a fine suit to wear to his execution and enough money to purchase some peanuts, candy and other small items. Most sources say that the deal was cut with Dr. W.E. Pattison of Westport

The actual noose used to hang Henry. *Courtesy of the Collection of Adirondack History Center Museum/Essex County Historical Society. Photo by author.*

and that the good doctor was kind enough to buy the suit for Henry and deliver it straight to the jail. However, the *Ticonderoga Sentinel* ran an article on May 11, 1933, called "More Sidelights on County's Last Hanging," which raised questions about who the corpse was actually given to, after a respected Ticonderoga dentist named Dr. H.E. Douglass came forward to set the record straight and announced that it was he and another unnamed doctor who had purchased the body for dissection in a room they had rented for that purpose in Westport.

Executed!

I see my brother. He is in this audience.

—April 27, 1883

Father Redington, a Catholic priest from Elizabethtown, was Henry's spiritual counselor in jail. On the morning of the execution, just after Henry made his final confession (which did not include the murder, for which he claimed innocence until the bitter end), he and Redington were joined by Fathers Butler, Devlin and McKeown from Ticonderoga, Keeseville and Massachusetts, respectively. It was reported that Henry—who had studied for the Catholic priesthood in France—actually served Holy Communion to the other priests that morning. The priests later quoted him as saying, "The judgment I am to meet today fades away in the light of the judgment I am to meet tomorrow." Redington rejected the idea that Henry was an infidel (nonbeliever), as was commonly assumed, and said that he and the other priests were hopeful for his soul.

According to the *Ticonderoga Sentinel* in an article from 1933, Henry loathed ex-sheriff Olcott because Olcott was the one who actually arrested him for murder and who fervently desired to spring the trap at Henry's execution. But Henry wouldn't give him that satisfaction. He told county officials that he would have to be carried to the gallows if Olcott was granted his wish. So Olcott instead would be given the "second-best" job: pulling the cap over Henry's head. Henry promised to "take [his] medicine like a man" if Undersheriff Jenkins was assigned the final task of sending him to his doom—a promise that would soon be fulfilled. He found Jenkins to be a fair and decent man during his imprisonment (even if the compliment was never to be returned) and even spent some of the money he made from the sale of his body to buy presents for Jenkins's children, according to Dr. Douglass.

Next on Henry's itinerary the morning of his execution was an inspection of the gallows for which Jenkins had A.F. Woodruff of Elizabethtown fashion a trapdoor type he had seen used at an execution in Windsor, Vermont. Thus, at nine o'clock that morning, a freshly shaven, sharply dressed Debosnys—cigar in mouth—approached the scaffold like a businessman on a mission. According to a *New York Times* article dated April 28, 1883, when asked if he needed help ascending the steps, he responded haughtily, "I can go up quicker than you," and up he went.

> *He took the noose in his hand, and, after examining it, he expressed the opinion that it would not work well and requested the Sheriff to soap the rope* [for lubrication]. *Then, taking his position on the trap, he looked around him and said: "Is this where I stand? I hope my head won't strike that fence when I go down." On being asked how he felt, he replied with a laugh: "There are many men more sick today than I am." He returned to his cell, and to the priest who attended him he protested his innocence.*

The few reporters and officers who accompanied him for the unusual inspection said he asked Jenkins to make sure there was plenty of slack in the rope, all the while laughing aloud—perhaps for the sake of the crowd he suspected had hoped to see him suffer and squirm at the end. Instead, he bowed to those bystanders who had already arrived for the event and shook hands with a couple whom he recognized. But when he returned to his cell—away from the spotlight—he sat down and cried. Father Redington asked him why, and he replied that he had just seen his brother, whom he didn't identify, outside in the crowd. Lehagaret? Had the man returned to see his brother off on his final journey? How did he get one of the tickets to the "show," unless he was still living in the county?

Standing around the scaffold in the northeast end of the gated jail yard were about seventy-five witnesses, including officers of the law and reporters. But on the commons on the periphery of the jail yard stood approximately *two thousand* people who had traveled into town that morning from nearly every town in Essex County. This was, after all, only the second (and thankfully the last) hanging the county had ever witnessed, and it was certainly the most famous murder case in its history. But the hordes of

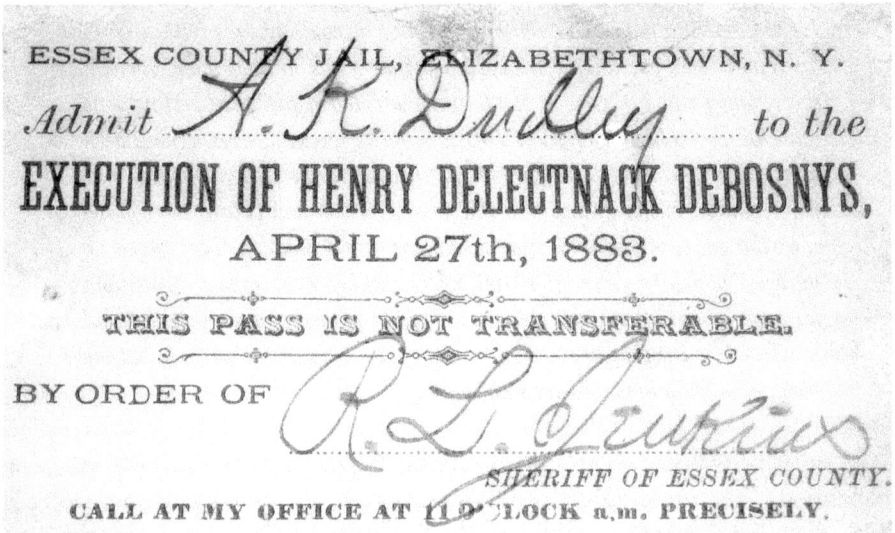

An authentic ticket to the famous hanging. *Photo by author. Courtesy of the Collection of Adirondack History Center Museum/Essex County Historical Society.*

ticket holders would only be able to see Henry's head and shoulders before his body fell through the trapdoor in the scaffold.

It seems as if every newspaper at the time had a different version of exactly what Debosnys's last words were: "I die innocent," "It was the blood of a chipmunk," "I see my brother," etc. But they all agreed that about quarter to noon on that cold, dreariest of days, Henry was led from his cell to the gallows, accompanied by the four priests to whom he had served Communion earlier that morning. His step was firm, as it had been on the practice run earlier, and he proceeded directly to the position he was to assume on the drop. Since the death warrant had already been read to him inside the jailhouse, he was asked if he had anything else he wished to say (implying, perhaps, a deathbed confession). According to some sources, all Henry could offer was that the blood on his knife really had been that of a chipmunk he had killed but that he was nevertheless prepared to die. The *Plattsburgh Republican* of May 3, 1883, clearly expected an admission of guilt or at least a show of remorse:

> *The most shocking circumstance was the fact that when asked if he had anything to say, the prisoner protested his innocence of a crime of which there does not seem to be a shadow of doubt he knew he was wholly guilty.*

He remarked to the priests while in jail that he could not die with a lie in his mouth, and yet this is precisely what he seems to have done. In fact, everything he has uttered from the time he deluded his unsuspecting wife with his Port Henry story, to the last words he uttered, seems to have been a mesh of falsehoods. The story of his life, which we have published, may have contained some grains of truth, possibly much that is true, but coming from the source it did, it must be considered very unreliable. The "secret of his life," which he was to give [us], will probably never appear. Aside from his protestation of innocence, the only remark made by him on the scaffold was a statement that the blood on his knife was not human blood, but the blood of a chipmunk which he had killed!

As the rope was drawn around Henry's neck, some papers reported that he exclaimed, "It's a little tight, but I don't suppose you will keep me here long!" With that, Jenkins tapped the spring that "hurled Debosnys to eternity," as the *Ticonderoga Sentinel* so aptly put it. At the same time, a man in the crowd fainted, and a newspaper hinted that it must have been Henry's brother whom he had mentioned earlier to the priest. Dr. Douglass, the dentist, was a medical student in Westport at the time, and he recalled that he and the doctors examining the body postmortem discovered that Henry had actually died "from strangulation upon the gallows" and not from a broken neck as was widely believed (and is typically the case in hangings). The hangman's knot that Henry allegedly complained about after the hood was drawn over his head was, in fact, pulled too tightly around his neck before the execution was even carried out. In that scenario, he was dead *before* the drop was sprung, which would explain how he died without so much as a twitch of his limbs (ironically, just what he had hoped for). So those who expected to see him suffer and squirm were the ones left hanging—pun intended. Knowing all of this, read again a few selected lines from the aforementioned poem called "Poor Henru":

As my enemies would like, I imagine
To see me go trembling like a child
Straight to the scaffold like a poor victim—
Of the lies of the poor wretched inhabitants
To give them this pleasure would be great folly
And supposing the joy that they feel in advance
I give myself the pleasure of laying aside my life
Into the funereal hands of death with confidence

Leaving for my judges the absent murderer.
Minute research will lead I hope
To the true guilty one who will take my place in the judgment
Since, for a foreigner like myself, they have no sympathy.

Henry's execution had gone off just as he had planned; when all was said and done, Jenkins and some twenty deputies were commended by the news media for the fine job they did controlling such an immense crowd. One paper noted, "The most perfect order and quiet was maintained throughout." Besides the usual correspondents from the local scene, reporters had been dispatched from Troy, Albany, Glens Falls, Ticonderoga, Burlington and New York City. The *New York Times* ran its story on the execution in the next morning's paper:

> *The procession to the gallows formed at 11:45 o'clock. DeBosnys, before the black cap was drawn over his face, said: "Gentlemen, I thank you for your many acts of kindness. I am innocent of the crime for which the law has condemned me to death. If there was blood on my knife, it was not my wife's blood. I die innocent." Under-sheriff Jenkins adjusted the noose and DeBosnys took his place on the trap. Ex-Sheriff Olcott put on the black cap, and at 11:52 o'clock Sheriff Jenkins said: "May the Lord have mercy on your soul," and sprang the trap.*

Doctors Bailey and Turner pronounced the alleged wife killer dead when his pulse had finally ceased sixteen minutes later. A half hour after the execution had commenced, ex-sheriff Talbot loosened the rope to release the body so that it could be examined by physicians before being turned over to the rightful party. That's when they found tattoos literally covering the deceased's body; apparently, they were too explicit to describe in the local press in those days. One news article speculated that the tattoos could be the "secret of his life" that he said would be known upon his death. And the *Gazette* of May 3, 1883, said, "The tattooing on the limbs of Debosnys was revolting enough to make even the remembrance of one so vile disgusting to the minds of decent people." "Small-town USA" wasn't quite ready for such risqué designs at that time, so the shock value was off the charts when that particular "secret" was revealed. Such tattoos were actually very popular in Europe at the time and likely held good, solid clues to Henry's background. For example, in 1861, after a French surgeon named Maurice Burchon penned an award-winning medical paper about the deleterious effects of tattooing, the French navy and army banned tattooing. Henry was affiliated with various French military branches, we would later learn. But, unlike in his native France, where prison officials recognized the value of keeping detailed records of the tattoos on each convict as early as 1808, nobody in Essex County bothered to take the time to carefully record the images found on Henry's body before his flesh was removed and disposed of. So any pertinent information about his identity that could possibly have been revealed by those tattoos was lost forever. After the body was examined one last time, it was placed in a rough coffin and kept in jail until nightfall, when a couple of doctors would receive the remains to dispose of as they saw fit.

The Paris press made its favoritism of Debosnys apparent in an article published in the *New York Sun* in July 1883: "The Parisian press has been greatly puzzled by the circumstantial accounts given in American newspapers of the life and ignominious death of a French adventurer who was hanged April 27th at Elizabethtown." Circumstantial accounts? Ignominious death? It's as if the French press felt that Debosnys's guilt was questionable in this matter and that the punishment dealt him for the murder was not only too harsh but also too humiliating, disgraceful and reprehensible—as if the murder of his wife had been just a minor offense. The *New York Times* tended toward that same sentiment with a story it ran the day after the execution called "A Remarkable Man Hanged. The Adventurous Life of a Soldier of Fortune Ended on the Gallows."

HENRY DELETNACK DEBOSNYS
(SO-CALLED)

My downfall will never reach a member of my family in this world!
—Henry Debosnys, April 12, 1883

Besides the extraordinary facts of his life, there is a good deal of mystery about the man. DeBosnys is merely an assumed name, and what his real name is no one knows, nor, from the present outlook, ever will know. The murderer is extremely reticent about his personal antecedents, his family and his friends. Since his arrest, he has communicated only with the French Consul at New York, but of course that official could do nothing to shield him from the consequences of his crime. At the time of his trial, DeBosnys was very sick and had to be taken into court. He listened to all the proceedings with an air of the most complete indifference—an indifference which disappeared only at the passing of the death sentence, when the wretched man broke down and wept and sobbed aloud. He subsequently attempted to starve himself to death, but the jail authorities frustrated the attempt...His time he spends in writing his autobiography, and a singular document it must prove to be. Altogether, it is a most extraordinary case and DeBosnys is a most extraordinary man.
—Burlington, Vermont, April 17, 1883

It was no secret that "Henry Debosnys" was an alias—that was one thing he had been vehemently upfront about from the start. Determined to save face for his family's sake, he had no intention of anyone finding out his true identity until well after his children had lived out their natural lives. But there were plenty of revelations in the hastily penned autobiography that he crafted while in jail. One wonders if Betsey Wells would still have said "I do" had she known of his colorful past: that he never remained in one place for too long, regardless of marital status; that two of his previous wives had died young—one presumably of starvation and the other a victim of an "accidental" drowning; that he had an insatiable appetite for fighting in wars; or that he was writing love poems to his first two wives when he should have been grieving the loss of Betsey. And what must the respectable widow have thought when they consummated their marriage and the "disgusting" tattoos covering her new husband's body were revealed to her for the first time? Yet, for all his faults—and there were many—he obviously could turn on the charm (in spades) when necessary, as Betsey Wells and his first two wives discovered too late. He was extraordinarily well-read and a gifted linguist, speaking and writing six languages fluently; the cryptograms and pictographs he created were certainly intriguing. But what was the purpose of a secret code? What was he hiding? If the detailed timeline of his life, as he meticulously recorded, is to be believed, then either his memory was nothing short of extraordinary for dates, places and events, or like a seasoned military officer of the time, he kept a careful daily journal of his activities and had access to that journal in jail.

When I first read Henry's sketches of his remarkable life, I thought to myself, there's no way—no *way*—he could ramble off all those dates, places and events so easily. They had to be contrived, I thought, as do most who read them the first time. Much to my astonishment, when I began researching the information to see if any dates matched up with actual battles, for instance, or with foreign schools known then by a different name than they are today, I discovered that he was right on the mark and historically correct in every detail. Once again, I found myself saying "no *way*," only this time it was because I couldn't believe that he was able to jot down this information, accurately, from his jail cell, from memory and without any history books or encyclopedias to use for reference.

Was he some kind of savant? Kim Peek, the famous savant on whom the movie *Rain Man* was based, could recall "almost everything he read, memorizing vast amounts of information…from history and literature, geography…and dates," according to his entry on Wikipedia. Savant syndrome is a rare condition in which individuals exhibit one or more areas of brilliance beyond average or even above-average human ability; however, there is usually a tradeoff in that many of these individuals have some type of autism or mental disability that is either congenital or caused by brain injury. In the latter case, there has also been a connection between epileptic fits presumably exacerbated by the brain injury and savantism. Henry had a history of epilepsy, as well as a known head injury from a battle wound suffered at Gettysburg in 1863. Could that injury have been the trigger of savant syndrome causing him to, from that point on, remember every intricate detail of his life as if he were an outsider reading it detachedly from an encyclopedia?

More convincing in this theory was the fact that each time he was asked about his past, both before and after he put it all down on paper in one place, he gave the same immediate and concise answers—entirely from memory. He didn't say, "Let me look it up and get back to you." Robert Hall, in a 1962 *Valley News* special edition, said that Henry's history was fictitious and that he had "constructed...an imaginary past" that included a noble lineage and strong relationships with each of his wives. I have to respectfully disagree. After months of exhaustive research, I found that his background, with the exception of his true identity, and his alibis (like the French Consul and the French Society in New York City and Philadelphia) check out. There were local business owners who recalled Henry painting for them in Essex in the early 1870s, when he said he had lived there for a short time with wife Celestine.

Debosnys illustration in the jailhouse Autographs book. *Courtesy of the Collection of Brewster Memorial Library/Essex County Historical Society.*

Had such a voluminous history been fabricated, Henry would have tripped over the myriad details in an attempt to keep them straight, but he didn't. His answers were always the same. This was a revelation to me. Maybe he *did* tell the truth more often than we've given him credit for (even if that virtue failed him in regards to the murder of his third wife). When describing his participation in the Franco-Prussian War, for example, he writes that he fled to Brussels, Belgium, after being sentenced to be shot for refusing to turn over four hundred guns in his care to the Commune of Paris. He spent two weeks in Belgium and then returned to Paris and Havre de Grace before embarking on the *Cimbria* for New York. So I Googled the *Cimbria*, and sure enough, there was such a ship on the Hamburg-America Line by Caird & Co. It was in service from 1867 until it sunk in a deadly collision in 1882. Therefore, it was active in the 1870–71 timeframe during which Henry claims to have sailed on it, and its route took it from Hamburg (305 miles southeast of Belgium) to Havre de Grace, where it picked up passengers before continuing on its last leg of the journey to New York City. It was not only possible but probable that Henry had, in fact, returned to New York City on the *Cimbria*, just as he had stated. Countless other facts that he listed, found in this chapter, prove historically accurate right down the most intimate details that would not have been found in history books at that time. As I dug deeper into the notes he left behind, checking each off as I verified it, I realized that Henry had been more truthful than previously thought. With the Internet as our ally, there has been no better time in history to prove, or refute, Henry's recollections.

The various "chapters" of Henry's life are listed below, as shown in the *Post & Gazette* of April 12, 1883 (when Henry dictated his notes to the reporters), and April 19, 1883 (when Henry handed the remainder of his notes over to the reporters to transcribe). He was obviously eager to share the better side of himself with those who believed he was nothing more than a murderer. This lengthy timeline of Henry's life is peppered with many unfamiliar foreign names and places, which I'm sure the reporters made every effort to spell phonetically. But I took the liberty to correct misspelled words discovered through my own research in order to assist future researchers. Proper grammar was applied, where needed, and abbreviations have been spelled out wherever possible for reader clarity. Read this section carefully, for herein lie countless clues.

We visited the County Jail Tuesday morning for the purpose of an interview with DeBosnys, he having expressed a desire for us to do so to Under-

Sheriff Jenkins. We found DeBosnys sitting at a table in the corridor of the lower floor in the new jail addition, busily engaged in writing. He was in good spirits and apparently perfect health. At his dictation, from a written copy before him, we wrote down the following:

"I was born May 16, 1836, at Belem, Portugal, on my uncle's plantation a few miles from Lisbon, on the shore of the Tagus River; removed to France with my parents in November 1836; removed to Havre de Grace in April 1838 and remained there until January 1839, when I went with my father to Giromaunt; attended the communal school of Giromaunt from 1843 to 1845. Removed from there to Compiegne College in June 1845 and remained until September 1847. Was with the North Pole Expedition under McClure from February 1848 to October 1850; at Paris from January 1852 to 1853; admitted to the College la Grande May 1853 to 1854; volunteered for the Crimean War with my father and one brother from June 1854 to 1856; admitted to the seminary of St. Brieuc (Cotes-du-Nord) July 1856 and remained until January 1858; at Normal Superior School at Paris from February to December 1858. Volunteered for Italian War in 1859 under MacMahon; embarked at Genoa for China under the Count of Palikao August 1859. In Pekin [Beijing] in 1860. In Mexico under Bazaine August 1861. Removed to Mexican side after Bazaine's treason. Captain of Guerillas under Lopez; wounded at Delpass Amidjo, June 7, 1862. In America February 1863, volunteered in 4th Pennsylvania under McIntosh; at Gettysburg July 1863, wounded in head and left hand with sword. Back to France in March 1864. Married in May 1864 to Miss Judith Desmarais. In the Arctic expedition from July 1864 to February 1867 under Captain Frank. Back to Rome in February 1867. Went to Paris in March 1868 and to New York in June 1868. Moved to the Indian Territory with the Osage tribe to Canville Creek on the Canadian river, and went back to New York June 1869. Volunteered for Franco-Prussian War in 1870 with 600 men from America. In France under General Bourbaki in October and General de Busseroles from October to November. I was Colonel under General de Busseroles engaged in skirmishing in December at Autin; drove the Prussians out of Nuit Sousbone 15th December, 3 o'clock A.M., and took the place, capturing 55 prisoners, arms and baggage. December 16th, Battle of Autin and capture of the road and stone bridge; 11 men and 2 horses killed; retreated to woods and lost 4 men. December 19th attacked advance guard on Autin Road, 4 Prussians killed and 7 prisoners; 8 Frenchmen killed. December 28 pursuit

Elaborate Debosnys sketch depicting his birthplace, the plantation of Belem. *Courtesy of the Collection of Brewster Memorial Library/Essex County Historical Society.*

of Prussian detachment of Hussars 'of the death,' and capture of 5 horses, 1 man and 1 wagon of provisions; January 1, 1871, St. Claude skirmish along the road; 4th and 5th January, Battle of Vergram; 6th and 7th January, Great March; 8th January, Battle of Maisondon by the whole army under General Bourbaki at Chateau with the 4th Company of Chasseur; Prussian retreat with heavy loss, 1800 prisoners; whole army pursued enemy to St. Marie. January 12 assault of Plateau de Montpellier, and capture of

*7 pieces of artillery and 50 prisoners, 21 men killed, 48 wounded, 3
cars burned. Retreat of General Bourbaki to Switzerland by the Pontavlier
Road and Verriere le Suisse."*

It's very important to mention here that on the original foolscap
documents from which this article was dictated, one titled "French War
1870" includes additional notes that Henry jotted down on the margin as
afterthoughts that were not included in the newspaper's published account
shown here. One of those notes said, "Change of name in October
[1870] and sent to the army of the Rhone, franc terror of the death under
Bourbaky and associated with the franck terror [*sic*]." So it sounds as if
Henry began using an alias in October 1870, and it had something to do
with his activities in the Franco-Prussian War when he was a colonel under
Bourbaki or de Busseroles. Another afterthought on that page mentions
"200 men of Henry embarked at Marseilles for New York, February 23,
1871." This would indicate that he sent the men under his command back
to the States just prior to the uprising in Paris. He doesn't say *he* went with
them. In fact, the last line on that page says, "Return of Col. Henry to
Marseille February to March, til [*sic*] the bombardment of the prefecture of
police" (the start of the Paris Commune), as dictated to the press below:

*"Return of Colonel Henry to Marseilles in March. Colonel Henry stayed
at Marseilles until after the bombardment of the Prefecture of the Police
by the fort St. Nicholas and Notre-Dame de la Garde, and the surrender of
Gaston Cremieux, the chief of the Commune of Marseilles; then returned
to Paris with 400 of his men—some of them volunteered in the regular
army at Versailles, some at St. Claude. Lived with his father in Paris
during the Commune and had 400 guns in his care which he refused to give
to the members of the Commune. He was [threatened] to be shot by the
generals Cluseret and Rosselle, in company of a man named Delescluze, for
refusing to take part in the Commune and deliver his guns. Colonel Henry
made some wood boxes and packed the guns and put them away in the cellar
of his house where the regular army of Versailles found them upon their
entrance into Paris. Colonel Henry was arrested and sent to Versailles; was
tried and sentenced to be shot the same day of the sentence, but he made
his escape through a platoon of 30 bayonets and went back to Paris to his
father; took 3,000 francs and then took the cars for Brussels, Belgium,
where he remained until all the errors of the sentence were corrected. He
then returned to Paris and went to Havre de Grace where he embarked on*

71

board the Cimbria for New York in June. His wife, Mrs. Judith Debosnys, died in July and her body was sent to France to be buried in her family vault; the father of the wife accompanied the body to France. She had given all her property to her children, except a little money which was placed on interest. Henry Debosnys went back to France every spring following and stayed a month or two with his family. He has two children, a daughter and a son; the daughter was 17 years of age in February 1883, and the son was 14 in October 1882; they live in England with a sister of Henry Debosnys; they are educated in English, French, Spanish, and German. The father and children of Henry Debosnys do not know of the downfall of today; his death will remain a secret to them. He leaves a house which, after the death of his father, goes to his two children. In 1871 Debosnys lost $9,000 worth of property, destroyed by fire on Grand Street, New York, in September; in August 1872 he went to Canada; in December he married Mrs. Celestine, his second wife, and in March 1873 they moved to Keeseville. In April came to Essex village and remained until July 1873; then to Burlington, Vermont, until August 27; in N.Y. from September to November 1873; in Philadelphia from December 1873 to November 1875; Omaha, December 1875 to May 1878. Left his farm in his brother's care and went with his wife to California in May 1876, and in September went to the Black Hills; there until October 1877; in May 1878 sold his farm and returned to Philadelphia, June 1879; at Wilmington, Delaware, October 1879 to May 1881. Death of Mrs. Debosnys (Celestine) March 5, 1882, in Philadelphia. Sold his place in Greenwich Point and came back to Essex village May 1, 1882. Married Elizabeth Wells June 8, 1882, and arrested August 1 for the murder of his wife and sentenced March 7, 1883, to be hanged by the neck on the 27th of April 1883.

'My history since 1871 until this day can be recorded without difficulty. I have all the references required to prove where I have stopped in each place mentioned in the index of my life; the references are in my trunk with some family papers (if not stolen). I have traveled more than I can write in this little recital. I keep some passages of my life so as to complete my family story. I could only give to you here a few words of my traveling and my occupation in this country. Am a good ornamental painter by trade and have worked in New York, Philadelphia, Chicago, New Orleans, Buffalo, and Albany; but I was a better trapper and lover of sport, and followed this last in preference to any other occupation. I went to the Indian Territory *as a trader with my uncle, and I have made a very good and independent living. But some accident, sickness and mortality pursued me, and I became poor. I had no friends because I never stayed long enough in the same place. I would have had plenty of friends if I was a man that loved the saloon and would pay a drink to any of the men that worked with me. As long as your money lasts, you have good friends, but when that is gone, your good friends are gone, too; such kind friends never were mine. I never had any bad company and never anticipated the property of others; if I be poor, I be poor by sickness. I don't say that I was the very best kind of man; no, but I never did harm to anybody; more false reports against me than anything else.'*

Henry Debosnys has a good education, conversant with six languages, reads and writes five fluently. He draws very well and passes for a fair artist; but he is not so fair as it is believed. He says he knows the value of such compliments, and he thanks the people of Essex County for their good judgment in this matter and for their good history they have built against him since he has been arrested. But that doesn't hurt his name, nor his own family—they never had any opportunity to find his family name. And he says he is ready to go to his grave; that death does not scare him at all.

For the present, he keeps a menagerie of living animals—he has got a little baby that cries, a donkey that brays and kicks, a dog that barks, a goat that bleats, a crow that caws, and a rooster that crows, all of which can be seen free of charge at Mr. Jenkin's Hotel [the jail].

The secret of his life will be printed after his death."

[The foregoing is copied from manuscripts furnished us by Debosnys. He says he will give us more of his history for our next issue. In explanation of his menagerie: he is a perfect mimic and afternoons, when locked in his cell, he opens his menagerie, mimicking the several animals and birds very perfectly.]

Henry said that all of the references needed to prove that he had been in each place he mentioned were kept in his trunk, along with his family papers. Which trunk? The trunk he had in jail or the trunk he left behind at the Wells cottage or elsewhere? If he was referring to one he left at the Wells cottage, it was destroyed, along with everything else that had belonged to him, by Betsey's survivors immediately after the murder. Understandably, they wanted to be rid of anything connected to her killer. But there may have been an actual diary or journal in the trunk of "family papers" (wherever it was) in which he kept track of the dates, events and places listed in his biography. Historians know that military leaders often kept comprehensive journals of their daily activities, and Henry said that he was a colonel and had fought in many battles. And we know that he had connections that saved his hide in Europe more than once. So it's likely that his name, when we finally figure it out, will be noted somewhere in the annals of France. And once we find the surname he spent the last decade of his life protecting, the reason for his anonymity will make sense.

As Henry recommended on the top margin of one of his documents, his notes should be "read and reread" by historians for details of military significance, especially those regarding the Franco-Prussian War and the War of 1870, for those hold insights that only an eyewitness could have provided. Although he didn't dwell on the Commune of Paris in May 1871 in his notes, Henry clearly was involved in it right up to his neck and fled back to America as quickly as he could because of it. Not only do all of the dates and locations check out in regards to the Commune, but the names of the many individuals he mentioned were also authentic, regardless of how large or small a part they played in France's bloodiest civil war. Sir Alistair Horne's *The Fall of Paris: The Siege and the Commune 1870–71* is an excellent source for names and dates of this pivotal event in Henry's life. Henry stated that he was sentenced to be shot but escaped through a command of thirty bayonets to Belgium, before returning to Paris, where he boarded the *Cimbria* back to America. This is precisely what many other countless individuals did at that chaotic time in France's history.

Henry's decision to hide the four hundred guns "Delecluse" needed to help arm the Commune at the start of the uprising—and the fact that the Versailles army then confiscated the weapons to use against the supporters of the Commune—resulted in a heavily lopsided, gory defeat of the insurgents. In fact, May 21, 1871, is called the "Bloody Week" (*La Semaine Sanglante*) in France's history. More people died that week, the week before Henry escaped to Belgium, than in the entire Franco-Prussian War or the Reign of Terror. And Henry Debosnys was there as a witness—and nonparticipant. He remained in Belgium for two weeks, until his name was cleared (presumably by connections in high places), and then he returned to Paris just long enough to catch the ship back to America. One month later, his wife Judith—mother of his young son and daughter—died in New York City. An early news article said that she was found drowned in a

Debosnys sketch of a family estate in England at which his children resided. *Courtesy of the Collection of Brewster Memorial Library/Essex County Historical Society.*

river, and Henry was considered a suspect but was never arrested. I wonder if her drowning was, instead, by the hands of someone her husband had wronged during the events in the Paris Commune. Because of his activities in France, he would always remain a wanted man by someone, somewhere. And perhaps that's why he chose to not say much about that regrettable period of his life. He did, however, offer further thoughts regarding his children and his current situation here in America and signed the following notation "Henrius Debosnius":

[Regarding the children] *They have a good education in English, French, German and Spanish, Both have a revenue of 600 dollars yearly, interest at 4 per cent from their mother, and a property in Paris France. Henry Debosnys daughter and son do not know nothing of the sad case and sentence of their father, and will never hear from, by the members of their family. One Brother E.A. Deletnack Debosnys leave in this country some were near Nebraska, or Texas. Henry had left to his care some property, when he was in the state of Nebraska, and went to California, January to May 1875; and September 1876 went to the Black Hills until October 1877. A farm of 160 acres (property of Henry D. Debosnys) was sold at Omaha for the sum of $600 cash, and H. Debosnys and wife came back to Philadelphia. Henry bought a fishing boat at Newburg, and hired the boat to a party from Atlantic City, N.J. for $20 monthly. At Wilmington, Delaware, he bought the sloop of Mr. Martinez Coollie for the sum of $157 in cash. This boat was hired by H.C. Hamlen of Camden. Those boats were for H.D. Debosnys' son; they gave a profit $50 a month during the fishing season; in the summer season they were used for the transportation of vegetables to the market of different places* [like] *Philadelphia, Rochester, and Camden, N.Y.*

I could only give you here a few words of my traveling and my occupation in this country, on account of my family's name and their present situation. Not because my life past has been dark. No. But it is only for my family and my friends. It is enough for me to suffer this degradation without leaving the dishonor upon my family. My downfall will never reach a member of my family in this world! Many curious and ignorant peasant farmers of Essex County spoke evil about me and built every kind of story against me, without any knowledge of my name or my relation. Such persons are worse than the criminal by their false reports from one place to another. "No timebo millia populi circumdantis me." I am not afraid of ten thousand such people that set themselves against me. In pace in idipsum dormiam, et requiscam.

A notable reference to Henry's heritage is made above. He mentions protecting his family name because of their "present situation." It's up to us to figure out what was meant by that. He further says the "peasant farmers" of Essex County were ignorant of his name and his "relation," which sounds very much like the lingo of someone from nobility. He does, in fact, speak of the various family estates in Portugal, France and England.

The next portion of Henry's autobiography concerned his family's property in "Giromond Village, Oise, France," from 1740 to 1870. In 1957, it was difficult to confirm some of the information Henry left for us to sort through. Deputy Sheriff William Davis, for example, when researching the so-called Debosnys estate in "Giromond, Oise, France" of which Henry so often spoke, said that he had been "unable to locate such a village." Today, at the stroke of a key, one can quickly find that there is, indeed, such a village, although the spelling has been changed to "Giraumont" in the Oise "department" of France. Henry's mention of the Clairoy Mountain in his notes below could only have been known to a local, which adds further credibility to his recollections. A search for "Clairoy Mountain" online comes up with absolutely no matches, which rarely happens today; however, there was a single hit for a place in France called the "Mount of Clairoy," which happened to be right in Henry's neighborhood. Quoted in a book about Joan of Arc, called *Jeanne d'Arc, maid of Orleans, deliverer of France*, which was reprinted in 1902, Joan spoke of the "lofty mountain" that provided good cover near Compiegne, France. You'll recall that Henry attended school at Compiegne College from 1845 until 1847 (when he was just nine to eleven years of age). This section ends in the middle of a sentence, so either Henry never finished writing it or the next page was lost or given to someone who has never come forward with it.

The present number represents a view of the residence of the Debosnys family in 1850, the residence or castle was built and furnished by Mr. Midole D. Debosnys in 1740. In its dimensions and ornaments, it is such a one as presents the characters and fortune of the family. It stands upon an elliptic plain, formed by cutting down the apex of a mountain; and on the east and north way, big hills; and on the south and west side, it commands a view of the prairies for a hundred miles and brings under the eye one of the boldest and most beautiful horizons in the world; while on the south it presents an extent of prospect, bounded only by the spherical form of the earth in which nature seems to sleep in eternal repose, as if to form one of her finest contrasts with the rude and rolling grandeur on the west. In the wide prospect, and scattered to the north and south, are several detached mountains which contribute to animate and diversify this enchanting landscape; and, among them, to the south Clairoy Mountain which is so interestingly depicted in his notes. From this point, the philosopher was wont to enjoy that spectacle, among the sublimest [sic] of nature's operations, the looming of the

Debosnys sketch of "Family Property, Giromond Village, Oise, Franc." *Courtesy of the Collection of Brewster Memorial Library/Essex County Historical Society.*

distant mountains; and to watch the motions of the plants and the greater revolution of the celestial sphere from this summit, too, the patriot could look down, with uninterrupted vision, upon the wide expanse of the world around for which he considered himself born; and upward, to the open and vaulted heavens to which he seemed to approach, as if to keep him continually in mind of his responsibility.

Approaching the tower on the southwest, the visitor instinctively pauses to cast around one thrilling glance at this magnificent panorama; and then passing to the hall where, if he had not been previously informed, he would immediately perceive that he was entering the house of no common man. In the spacious and lofty hall which opens before him, he marks no tawdry and unmeaning ornaments: but before, on the right, on the left, all around,

the eye is struck and gratified with objects of science and taste, so classed and arranged as to produce their finest effect. On one side, specimens of sculpture set out in such order as to exhibit at a coup d'oeil the historical progress of that art. From the hall he was ushered into a noble salon from which the glorious landscape of the west side again burst upon his view; and which within is hung thick around with the finest productions of the pencil—historical paintings of the most striking subjects from all sections of the country, and all ages: the portraits of distinguished men and patriots, both of Europe and America, and medallions and engravings in endless profusion. Few homes were more attractive and imposing than the castle where Mr. D. Debosnys and family were born. It possessed a very fine garden from which the most enchanting views were obtained of mountain, river, and valley. Part of it was arranged and most carefully kept as a bowling green. This lay on one side of the house and ran parallel with the high road from which it was separated by a hedge.

The best apartment of the entire building was appropriated to my father, mother, and sisters; and I was accommodated in a small apartment next to the kitchen, on the ground floor, with a window opening upon the bowling green.

One night it was unusually hot and close. We had retired early, according to my father's wont; but my room was so stuffy that I could not sleep or even rest, and after tossing about most uncomfortably for a long period, I got up. And putting on a few clothes, threw open the window and stepped out onto the bowling green. The night was exquisite; the full moon was shining in all her glorious splendor—it was, in fact, nearly as light as day. After walking about the garden, I returned to the bowling green and sat down in a pretty arbor covered with creeping plants. The air was soft and deliciously cool, and everything seemed to induce to calm enjoyment which was enhanced by the profound stillness that reigned around, broken only by the murmur of a distant waterfall. While thoroughly enjoying this beautiful scene, the village clock struck one, and I fancied I heard the sound of wheels and horses' feet approaching. In a short time I saw a vehicle come in sight and pass slowly along the high road; and, as my arbor was on the opposite side of the green, I could readily observe in the bright clear moonlight that it was a large family coach, such as country squires often drove drawn by two tall, fat horses and attended by coachmen and footmen in liveries and cocked hats. It turned the corner before mentioned to proceed through the village, as I supposed. Not so, however, for it stopped immediately, and I heard the door open and the steps let down and the sound of feet approaching the

Elaborate Debosnys sketch of unidentified male. *Courtesy of the Collection of Brewster Memorial Library/Essex County Historical Society.*

castle. "Belated travelers," thought I. "It's little use, your trying the King Head, for we certainly can't take you in." But this was not the intention of the party. It was not the castle but the big garden which they required; for they all stopped at the end of the bowling green furthest away from the castle, where the hedge happened to be very loose and thin. One of the party instantly pushed himself through, and walking a few steps into the green, stood still and looked carefully round. From my having been brought up entirely among soldiers, all military uniforms were perfectly familiar to me; and I therefore instantly recognized the huge gold-laced cocked hats, blue and green cloak, jack boots and spurs, and a heavy...

[Signed] *Henecos D. Debonostys*

In the next section, we see that Henry clearly admired his uncle, Captain Maurice Debosnys, and surely strived to be like him. His was clearly a military family. Unfortunately, the last sentence of the first paragraph is cut off (just when it was getting good) when Henry reached the end of the page he was writing on, so we'll never know who the blue-eyed, slender female figure was who greeted his uncle at the door. That portion of the story was likely written on another page that is long lost. Instead, the story of Maurice Debosnys jumps to a part regarding a fatal duel:

> Captain Maurice Debosnys of the Dragoon, came riding through the wood in a southerly direction, through the ruddy glow of the glorious sun of Giromond now nearing its setting, it glistened intermittently upon the sleek flanks of his horse, and touched the rider's thin, smooth cheek and black mustache. Handsome and gallant he looks, this tall young officer; and no man in the regiment had a braver record or fairer prospects than he. His social qualities were fully on a level with his warlike ones. He was merry and good-humored; a teller of capital stories, a strict disciplinarian, yet popular with his men; and inexhaustive [sic] getter-up of and leader in all sorts of diversions to relieve the monotony of camp; a man whom all women are apt to like, and a man who knew how to win a woman's heart gracefully such as he was, for good or evil. Captain Maurice rode through the wood that June afternoon until the trees thinned away, and Mansion House with a broad piazza and open windows, appeared on a slight elevation beyond. As he rode up to the door and flung himself out of the saddle, a Negro slave led away his horse, and Captain Maurice sprang up the steps of the piazza with a light foot. Before he reached the door, a slender figure, dressed in white with a blue sash around her waist and a bow of the same color in her hair, made her appearance on the broad threshold. Maurice Debosnys took both her hands in his, and looked smilingly into her eyes. Her eyes were blue... [hanging sentence]

> In all the papers of the country relating the story of the duel and describing the deceased very minutely and asking for information, the Spanish and the Portuguese embassies were communicated with and inquiries made as to whether any noble man or gentleman or rank was reported missing. All this was not only done, but a great deal more; and in the progress of time, answers were duly received from all the quarters. A letter from Lisbon, Portugul, claim[ed] the body of the deceased as the son of Mr. Maurice D. Debosnys, a rich man of Lisbon. As soon as the name was

Debosnys sketch of unidentified male, possibly his uncle, in the jailhouse Autographs book.
Courtesy of the Collection of Brewster Memorial Library/Essex County Historical Society.

pronounced, my father and my mother called at the Magistrate's office with the letters from Lisbon and claimed the body for the son of his brother. The magistrate and my father sent a telegram immediately to his brother Mr. Maurice D. Debosnys at Lisbon and invited him as relation to the deceased to come as soon as possible and make arrangements for the transportation of the dead body. Exactly one month after, my uncle was in the church vault accompanied by the magistrate, my father, the constable, and the coroner. My poor uncle, as soon as he see his dead son, that he kissed him again and again, my uncle showed to the magistrate a letter from his son, to his father at Lisbon telling the cause of the duel, and giving the name of his adversary in case of death, that he would claim for his body and his property, detail of the place for the duel, place unknown to him, and all the details for his superior officer of the squadron. My uncle asked the magistrate his advice for that matter; Lisbon is far away from here, and I believe it be better to leave the body in my brother's family vault and terminate all this mysterious affairs. The magistrate gave his approbation and [sent] for the arrestation.

A Parisian Chronicler's Tale

For what it's worth, when news of the hanging reached France, an anonymous "Parisian chronicler" felt compelled to submit a letter to the *New York Sun*, which then ran in the *Post & Gazette* on July 12, 1883. It is posted here in its entirety for your analysis. Personally, I challenge the chronicler's tale for a number of reasons. Nevertheless, in the interest of covering all bases, here is the "Keff" theory:

A Parisian Chronicler Guesses that His Friend Keff Has Been Hanged Here

The Parisian press has been greatly puzzled by the circumstantial accounts given in American newspapers of the life and ignominious death of a French adventurer who was hanged April 27ᵗʰ at Elizabethtown. He had murdered on the 1ˢᵗ of August 1882 his third wife, Elizabeth Wells. On his trial, he did not conceal the fact that Debosnys was a borrowed name. His real one would be found, he said, in his autobiography written in prison. All that need be known for the present, he said, was that after a brilliant course of studies in Paris, he had entered the Superior Normal School, where he had been intimately acquainted with Edmond About, Francisque Sarcey, and many others who have since been prominent in contemporary literature. He related that he had made two Arctic voyages and had been a soldier in the Crimea and in Mexico. Thereupon, a Parisian chronicler writes:

"I am positive that the so-called Henry D. Debosnys was my comrade Keff. I see him still, a good-sized fellow with long, black hair, a smooth, fat, always carefully shaved face emerging from a high white cravat; a very emphatic talker and elocutionist, especially when reciting his own verses; watching lovingly in the meantime the skillful blackening up of an old Marseilles pipe which he seemed to have been born smoking. For five years we met in Paris during the regular six weeks' vacation of the provincial colleges in which he was a teacher—the university not allowing him a stay of more than one scholastic year, whether in the north, the east, the west, the south, Corsica, or even Algeria, because he always ran into debt and kept company with tipplers. I have still in my panoply the pretty pocket pistol with a damascene butt which I lent to him three times to blow out what he called his brains, in consequence of three distinct failures in hunting rich heiresses. Keff showed me the last time I saw him the following letters:

'Mr. Keff: I've just found among my daughter's papers two letters, one of which is in very poor poetry, signed by you, and states that you are ready to elope with my Ginseppa on the horse of a certain Mazeppa, whom I suspect to be a licensed vender of Bastia/Corseca. The other is signed by a Mr. Peyrodal, a druggist's clerk now with his family in Cette. I warn you both that I give you two weeks to come and marry my daughter Ginseppa. So much the worse for the one who arrives second in the race. He is a dead man.

With much respect,
Brascatelli D'Istria
Non-commissioned officer in the Gendarmerie of Bastia.'

The other ran thus:

'My old fellow Keff: The Dominican Republic has entrusted me with the organization of its Department of Public Instruction, left by the infamous Solouque in a lamentable state of decrepitude. I need a true friend to help me. If you see fit to abandon Corsica, come at once.

Tibi, X.'

Keff said he was going to San Domingo and proposed to join the army there. 'I am sure,' he said, 'it is my true calling in this world. When young

I fought like a lion near Colonel de Montagne when we attacked Lidi-Brahim's marabous. I even remember that I fled wonderfully quick with Major Comby de Cagnord and his forty hussars and wrote on that affair a magnificent piece of poetry.'

'What nonsense, man! At that time you were only twelve years old and at Charlemagne with me.'

'You must be mistaken. I was at Lidi-Brahim, for I wrote verses about it.'

I did not insist, knowing well that it was his hobby to think he had been a witness of whatever he wrote verses about. I have not heard of him since."

Had Henry Debosnys been Mr. Keff, as this person suggested, wouldn't he have mentioned Lidi-Brahim, Colonel de Montagne, Corsica and Algeria in the exceedingly thorough notes of his travels? And there was no period of time when he remained in Paris teaching for five years straight, as the anonymous friend claimed. Furthermore, he was not really a "good-sized fellow," as described. At five feet, six inches tall, he was the average height of a man in the late 1800s.

THREE DEAD WIVES

She died so young and so cruelly, oh dear!
—Henry Debosnys, August 10, 1882

As impressive as Henry's autobiography is, if it's all true, there's still the sobering matter of the lives he took, namely Judith's, Celestine's and Betsey's. At least three times he was married to young, vibrant women, and each time the women associated with him ended up dead. Had he "arranged" the death of each of his wives when he no longer had use for them or when he realized he would not be getting a share of their property or wealth? Was his apathy toward human life the result of having spent nearly half his life in battle? What did all of the combat he saw do to his psyche?

In the case of Betsey's murder, many suspected that greed and revenge were motives. Greed, because Henry had been heard asking Betsey about the deed to her property as soon as they were married. And revenge, because she hadn't given it to him. He allegedly ransacked her home searching for the money she hid from the mining company settlement before her corpse had even turned cold. Finding nothing, he went in search of her daughters to see if they knew where it was. These are facts based on witness testimony. Betsey wasn't the first wife to leave Henry empty-handed upon her death. In his notes to the press, he mentioned that his first wife, Judith, to whom he was married from 1864 to 1871, left "a revenue of 600 dollars yearly, interest at 4 percent…and a property in Paris, France" to the children of that marriage, but nothing was left to Henry—at least nothing that he bothered to point out.

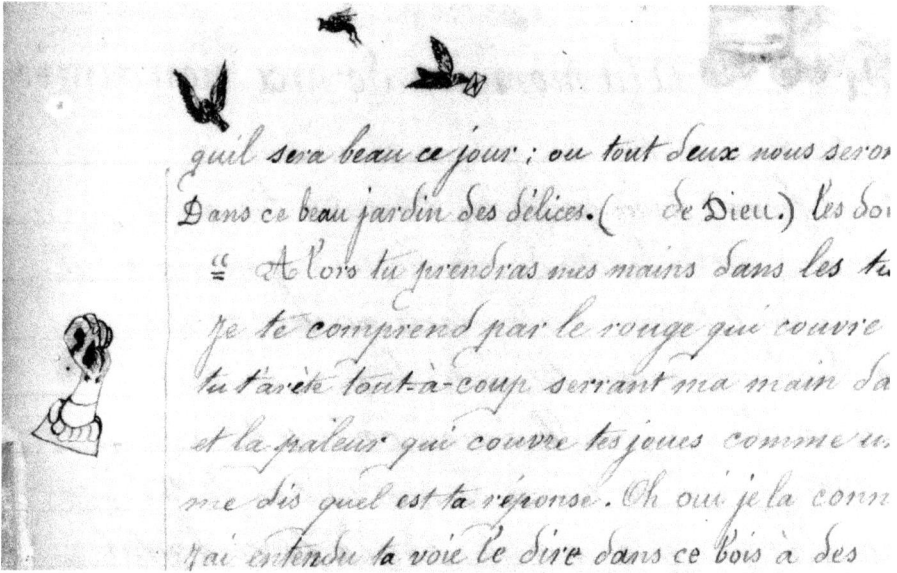

Portion of continuation of first poem Henry wrote following Betsey's murder. *Courtesy of the Collection of Brewster Memorial Library/Essex County Historical Society.*

The children to whom Henry alluded in his notes were a girl born in February 1866 and a boy born in October 1868. This means that his daughter was conceived in June 1865 between Henry's visit to the Arctic region and their trip to Rome. She would have been just five when her mother, Judith, died in New York City, and she was seventeen when, unbeknownst to her, her father was hanged in Elizabethtown. His son, mentioned with greater frequency, was conceived in either Rome or Paris in February 1868 and was not yet three when Judith passed away. The boy was fourteen years old at the time of his father's execution.

On January 12, 1883, the *Plattsburgh Sentinel* ran the following note regarding Judith Debosnys:

> *Ex-Sheriff Talbot recently received a letter from a Massachusetts party making inquiries in regard to DeBosnys. He states that he knew one Henry DeBosnys in Philadelphia, and that he left that city in company with a colored woman. He was suspected of murdering his first wife, by drowning in the Chiccasee [sic] river, and was nearly convicted.*

I've been unable to locate a river by that name in New York, Pennsylvania or anywhere else, but there's a good chance that the name of the river has changed in the past hundred years. There is, for example, a Chiques Creek in Pennsylvania that has been known by many variants, like Chickies Creek, Chicques Creek, Chiquesalunga Creek and so on. Perhaps the informant or sheriff was unsure of the spelling and attempted to spell it phonetically, in which case "Chiccasee" might pass for "Chicques." I wonder if the letter to Talbot mentioned the state in which the drowning allegedly occurred. I also wonder if that's truly how Judith Debosnys died, because I've been unable to find any news articles detailing her death—not even an obituary.

Or was the man who wrote to Talbot referring to Celestine, Henry's second wife, unaware that Henry was already a widower when he moved to Philadelphia with another wife? Interestingly, he never revealed the details of his wives' deaths or his feelings toward any of them in his written history. You would think the impact of such life-altering events would have warranted at least a tender mention of a loved one in one's memoirs, rather than lines like: "Death of Mrs. Judith Debosnys, July 1871, send to France for the funeral, placed in her family vault" and "Death of Mrs. Celestine Debosnys, March 5th 1882. Philadelphia. Back to Essex Village May 1st 1882." It seems that Henry was very guarded in the information he revealed about the most pivotal moments in his life, like the Paris Commune

Debosnys sketch, presumably of wife Judith. *Courtesy of the Collection of Brewster Memorial Library/Essex County Historical Society.*

and the passing of his wives. To his credit, however, he certainly wrote passionately about his wives in his poems.

Henry married his presumed second wife, a French Canadian named Celestine Desmarais, one year after Judith's sad demise. Celestine dutifully accompanied her restless husband on his countless moves to Keeseville and Essex (in 1873); Burlington, Vermont; Philadelphia, Pennsylvania; Omaha, Nebraska; and Wilmington, Delaware. They returned to Philadelphia in May 1881, and she died ten months later on March 5, 1882, allegedly of starvation.

According to the *Philadelphia Times* of August 11, 1882:

> *Debosnys is spoken of as a ne'er do well who loafed about the vicinity until forced by hunger to perform manual labor, which he could have had at any time in the oil mill. The French Society keeps a record of all moneys given to the needy French. In December 1878 appears an entry to Henri De Boisnys and wife, $2, and from that date on to March 9, 1882, when his wife Celestine died, De Boisnys's name constantly appears on the books as a recipient of charity. The Society, whose office is at 817 Arch Street, sent our reporter to Dr. Eugene T. Bernady. Dr. Bernady remembers Debosnys well*

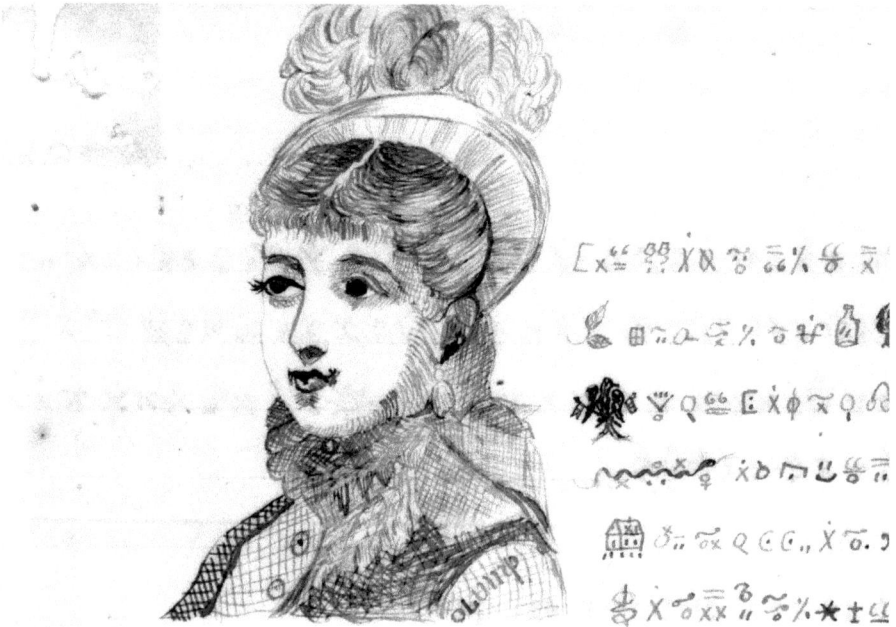

Debosnys sketch of female figure, presumably one of his wives. *Courtesy of the Collection of Brewster Memorial Library/Essex County Historical Society.*

and describes him as a man about five feet nine inches in height, thick and broad, of large build and evidently the possessor of great muscular strength. "He looked more like a brute than a man," said Dr. Bernady. "Never in all my experiences have I seen a worse face. He had a head shaped like that of the murderer Probat and a bad villainous eye. I could see nothing of the Frenchman about him except his language. He spoke excellent French."

It should be noted that on March 7, 1878, Celestine's doctor, funeral and burial expenses were paid for in full by the French Society. Her physician clearly wasn't impressed by Henry Debosnys, possibly blaming him for Celestine's starvation death. With the details of Celestine's interment out of the way, the unemployed widower—two times over—immediately hired a housekeeper to cook for him. Elizabeth Brown was a twenty-year-old "colored cook" known as "French Liz" or "Prue." When Henry decided to return to Essex County to again seek work as a painter, he offered to deliver Prue and her relatives to a farm in Newburgh aboard his "yacht." Prue later told the press, who caught up with her in Philadelphia before the authorities did, that once she was aboard the so-called yacht alone with Henry, it became clear to her that he had no intention of dropping her off in Newburgh, as he had agreed. The *Elizabethtown Post*, nine days after Betsey's murder, ran an article about Prue called "Debosnys Suspected of Another Murder."

About four months ago, Debosnys suddenly appeared in Essex Village. He had come by yacht and is reported [to have] been accompanied by a young, colored woman who posed as his wife. After residing in Essex a short time, Debosnys took the woman and her trunks in the yacht and went away. He was seen the next day having her trunks but claimed the woman worked in a laundry in Burlington; but this colored woman has not been seen in these parts, and though many people claim Debosnys drowned her in the lake, all this is but conjecture, and it is being investigated by the authorities.

On August 17, 1882, the *Essex County Republican* ran a follow-up article called "Missing Colored Cook Found in Philadelphia":

The name of the missing colored woman in the Debosnys murder mystery is Elizabeth Brown, alias "French Liz," and she has reappeared at her home in Philadelphia. She is twenty years old and lives in a miserable shanty formerly occupied by Debosnys on South 1ˢᵗ Street [now South Front Street] near Greenwich Point in the Quaker City. She became housekeeper for Debosnys after the death of his wife in March of this year. Debosnys and his wife had come to Philadelphia from Canada in a flatboat in the summer of 1880. "French Liz" was surprised to find her testimony was needed and laughed when told she was supposed to have been murdered.

She informed the police Debosnys had promised to take her and relatives to a farm in Newburgh. She went on the yacht thinking he would send it back for the family. The police assume the yacht was an old boat Debosnys had picked up or stolen. On this boat he rigged a sail and started for Canada, where he had friends. He constantly quarreled with the colored girl, and after passing Newburgh, he told her he was headed for Canada. She objected and asked to be put ashore, but somehow he managed to keep her on board, for it was not until he reached Charlotte on the Vermont side of Lake Champlain, across from Essex, New York, that he put her ashore and gave her fifty cents and told her to go to Burlington.

Henry wasted little time grieving. Just three months after Celestine's passing, he somehow weaseled his way into Elizabeth Wells's life and convinced the lonely widow to marry him. Only *three months* had elapsed between Celestine's death and his acquaintance and marriage to Betsey. Three months. That's all Celestine was worth to him. Regardless of the facts, his poems to and about each—written during his final imprisonment—reveal a seasoned widower, shameless in his professions of love to his three wives. They were written when a truly innocent man would have been grieving his most recent loss. Under any other circumstances, one might read the poems that follow and see simply pain and longing for lost loves; but in light of the circumstances surrounding Betsey Wells's death, they seem incredibly disrespectful to her memory and perhaps to the memory of Celestine and Judith Debosnys, as well.

From what I can tell, the very first document Henry created in jail following his arrest was written in French and was about Elizabeth. He numbered the upper left corners of most of his documents, and this one was numbered "1." The accompanying illustration depicts a man alone on a wagon, just as Henry was when he left the scene of the crime. I find it both interesting and disturbing that inside the wagon appears to be a body laid out on the buckboard. The poem was continued on the flipside of that document, a portion of which is shown at the start of this chapter. On that side, Henry illustrated it with a woman's raised fist, which appears to be bloodied, just as Betsey's was reported to be. Starting with that poem, "In Memory of My Love," which was written immediately after Betsey's murder, I give you the collection of Debosnys's love poems:

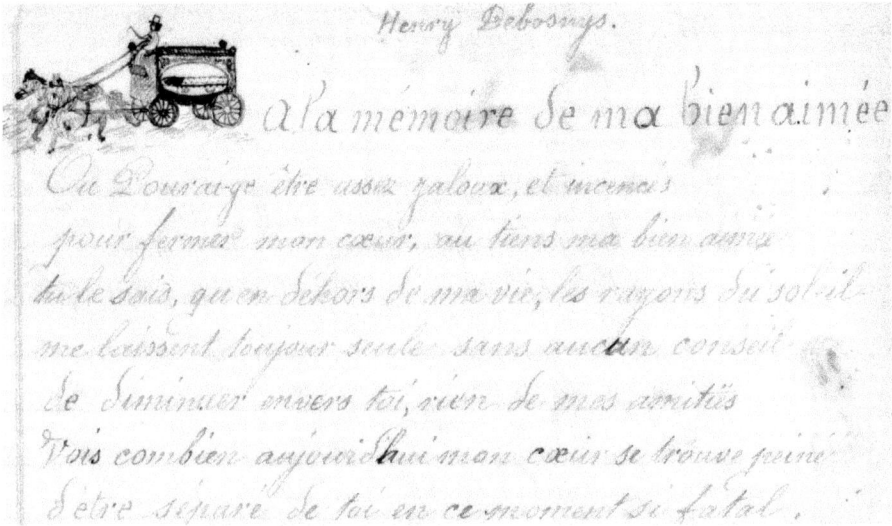

Portion of first poem Debosnys wrote in jail following Betsey's murder. *Courtesy of the Collection of Brewster Memorial Library/Essex County Historical Society.*

Or can I be jealous enough and angered
To close up my heart, (as for) thine, my dearly beloved
Thou knowest that outside of my life the rays of the sun
Leave me always alone without any counsel
To diminish toward thee, nothing of my friendship
See how troubled my heart is today
To be separated from thee in this so fatal moment
Which causes me to be treated with brutal force
Especially when under the phantoms of thy sad death…
Which ceaselessly appears in my mind
And which is for me a most unhappy lot.
Thy sweet blue eyes by me are not dulled
Nor thy mouth which breathed only for me
Before the day of that terrible jolt!
Without seeing me again and without taking thy last adieus
Thou didst leave me
Thou didst leave this earth to go to another world
Leaving on me all the responsibility
For which today, though innocent, I must answer.
Oh, if thy heart inclines toward me, go also toward my judges
Tell them how the event took place in my absence
For in my prison I have not a friend

ADIRONDACK ENIGMA

Who in the day of my judgment might prove my innocence
However it may be, my very dear and well-beloved
For thee I could suffer as a true prisoner
Hoping that upon leaving this earth I might again have thy friendship
Thy charming smile seen through my penitence
Gives me the strength and courage to go to rejoin thee
This time at least to be humiliated no more in this world
How beautiful will be that day when we two will be without sorrows
In that beautiful garden of delight, sweet privileged ones of God.
Then thou wilt take my hands in thine,
I understand thee by the blush that covers thy face
Thou dost suddenly stop, clasping my hand in thine
And the pallor that covers thy cheeks like a cloud
Tells me thy answer. Oh, yes, I knew it!
I have heard thy voice tell it in this wood to the shadows
To the bluebirds who repeat it in their songs so gay
As also each morn the thrush sings it to the world
The years will pass, that is the greatest truth
Yes, side by side we will sit all the days to come
And thousands and thousands of times the flowers will bloom;
Of our past
We will forget the springtime buds which in the future
Will not cease to flower in our thought.
Oh then, my dear beloved, God alone to serve
Will be our joy and our happiness in that great city
Where the reign of our eternal father will be forever
In my prison a place so black to see
When comes the evening I read with piety
For the Lord our God a humble collection
Of prayers, very sincere, on the present and on the past.

He who writes this poor sad story
No longer has, alas, that fair dear liberty
In his prison he aspires now only to the glory
That a God so justly good has reserved for us.

—August 1882

The next poem, numbered "2" in the top corner, was also translated from Henry's French.

Hope—Faith

Alas, my dear friends, it is surprising how shadows
Have enveloped my half-developed childhood
I hardly know that I am in this world
Since she whom I loved is among the dead.
But however before God I am consoled,
Since toward me she cast a sweet look of friendship
And her lips which appeared to smile in the shadow
Remain mute with a strange surprise without speaking?
Her sole desire here below was to appear before God
For the eternal rest for which she aspired in quitting this world!
The accused, the heavy-hearted, I often repeat.
My poor heart, you suffer in silence
Yes, you do well to guard your secret
If to the fortunate you show your suffering
Would they understand your suffering, your regrets
Oh, guide me but be not so tender,
Lest your outbursts be confined
From false speech you must defend yourself
My poor heart you must still hope.
My poor heart you must still hope.

Do you remember that under a charming smile
They hid from you infamous treasons
That their sweet transports were only a delirium
When came intoxication, your reason strayed
All your friends fled away like a dream
With all their flattery made to charm you
All their reports are only lies
My poor heart, you must still be patient.
I no longer wish for a hope that intoxicates
Of that happiness which endures for too few moments.
But can one live here below without hope—
No, for without it, life is without springtime.
Like a flower I know how to brave the storm.

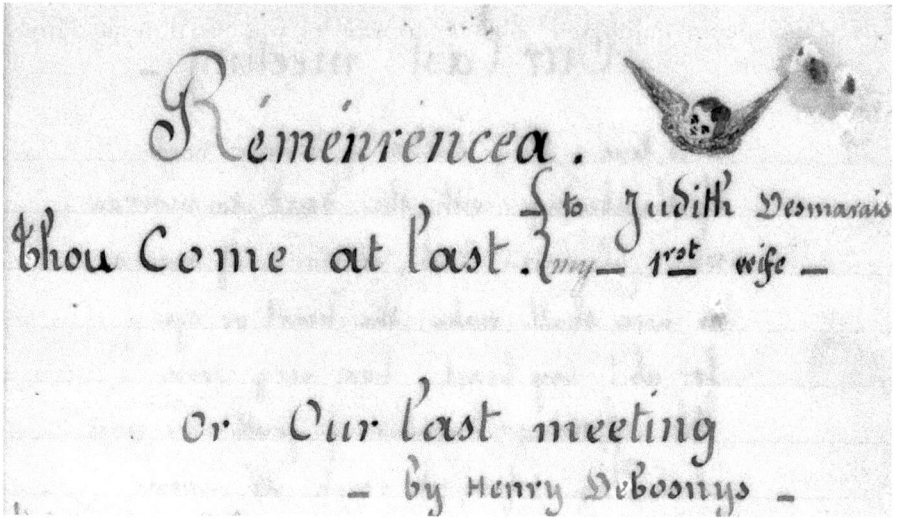

"Remembrance" by Debosnys, written for first wife, Judith. *Courtesy of the Collection of Brewster Memorial Library/Essex County Historical Society.*

Like a flower also I wish to revive,
All fair days are not without clouds
My poor heart, you must persist.

I have waited long, and my eyes are dim
With waiting and watching for thee my first love!
The moon sinks under the ocean's rim,
And a cloud floats over the sky above,
But thou hast come at last for I see
Thy slender figure, both little and tall,
And I hear the rustle of thy garments free.
Ah, it is thou, my dear Judith, near this wall
O, why hast thou tarried, my dear love so long
Yet art thou come to me here at last,
I hear thy voice and I know thy song
That have pleased us, in the past
Thy gentle eyes, gaze upon me
With tearful as I saw them some years last
Thy deep voice calls me, and thy hands beckon,
From the shadows of the past.

But we wander no more in sunlight
And we are singing no more in the moonlight.
Thou must have found many loved faces
Of old friends—in Heaven, thy now place.

———

Our Last Meeting

It is true, they talk of danger nigh
Of slumbering with the dead tomorrow,
Where pleasures throb, or tears of sorrow
No more shall wake the heart or eye.
For ah! my heart, how very soon
The glittering dreams of youth were past!
And long before it reached its noon
The sun of my poor life is overcast,
Glad with the beautiful evergreen summer,
Forever the splendor of the sun everlasting
With all our friends of other days forever
We will sing the immortal song of the Holy King?

—Henry Debosnys

———

Oh, but to see that head recline
A minute on this trembling arm,
And those mild eyes look up to mine
Without a dread, a thought of harm!
With that triumphant look faith wears
When not a cloud or fear or doubtz
To witness the young vernal burst
Of nature though those blooming spheres,
Those flowers of light that sprung beneath
The first touch of the eternal's breath

Debosnys sketch, presumably of wife Celestine. *Courtesy of the Collection of Brewster Memorial Library/Essex County Historical Society.*

It was my doom still to be haunted
By some new wonder, some sublime
And matchless work, that for the time
To know what shapes, so fair, must feel
To look, but once, beneath the seal.
By which the whole fond sex is led
Mingled with what I durst not blame.
It is not to be told how long,
How restlessly I sighed to find
Some one, from out that shining throng,
Some abstract of the form and mind
Of the whole matchless sex from which,
In my own arms beheld possessed.
I might learn all the powers to [which]

To warm and if my fate unblessed
Would have it ruin of the rest!
Days, months passed and though what most
On earth I sighed for was mine, all.
What happiness it is for those who fall
It was bitterest anguish made more keen
In agonizing cross light given
And made to light the conquering way
Of proud young beauty with their ray,
Oh! beautiful, or grand and strange
As quickly as you I wish I could change,
The mystery of that fountain-head,
And all breathe of life and fall with the dead.

"Read and Read Again," another poem and illustration for Celestine. *Courtesy of the Collection of Brewster Memorial Library/Essex County Historical Society.*

Thou have bid me happiness, and bid me adieu—
Can happiness live when absent from thou?
Will sleep on my eyelids ever sweetly alight,
When greeted no more by a tender good night?
Oh, never, for deep is the record enshrined;
Thy look and thy voice will survive in my mind:
Though age may the treasure of memory remove,
Unfading shall flourish the day of our love
Through life's winding valley in anguish, in rest
Exalted in joy, or by sorrow depressed;
From its place in the mirror that lies on my heart
Thine image shall never one moment depart.
When time, life, and all that poor mortals hold dear

Like visions, like dreams, shall at least disappear,
Though raised among seraphs to realms above
Unfading shall flourish the last day of love.
Oh! take though this young rose, and let her life be
Prolonged by the breath she will borrow from thee!
For while over her bosom, they soft voice shall thrill
She will think the night-bird is courting her still?

—By Her Husband Henry Debosnys
She died in Philadelphia
March 4th 1882

———◆———

Debosnys sketch of unidentified
woman, perhaps Celestine, in the
Autographs book. *Courtesy of the*
Collection of Brewster Memorial Library/
Essex County Historical Society.

March 5, 1882
Oh, my dear Celestine, I long for
death—
For anything I wish to be with thee
I did not inhale, alas thy dying breath,
That it might have power on me
To make me what thou art but thou art
dead
And I am here it strengthened me instead
My dear Celestine, joy, here is none.
It went into the grave with thee
And, grief, because my spirit is alone
Is all that come to comfort me.
The very air I breathe is turned to sighs,
And all my soul is wilting from my eyes
Oh my dear Celestine day after day
I seek thee, but thou art not near
I sat down on thy grave in the cold clay
And listen for thy soul—Oh dear—
And when some withered leaf falls
from the tree
I start as if thy soul had spoken to me.

—By Her Husband Henry Debosnys

100

The interesting thing about the next poem, "My Wife Last Home," is that Henry wrote the same poem on three different documents, each with a different image on top of the page. One has Betsey's daughters weeping at her tombstone, which says, "To Their Poor Mother E. Debosnys." One shows Betsey's tombstone beside a rather graphic heart and sun. And one (drawing no. 5) shows a little goat standing in front of a vine-draped tombstone bearing Betsey's name. The quality of the third image was too poor to reproduce, but the other two images are shown here. This is the only poem of which I'm aware that Henry wrote and illustrated more than once:

> *She died so young and so cruelly, oh dear—*
> *Her fleeting life was so speedily,*
> *She died murdered and not a friend was near*
> *To soothe there for her a dying bed,*
> *Alone without a single friend on foreign clime*
> *Around her weeping throng*
> *There her last tears dropped and she died,*
> *Alone take her, o god of the immortals*

One of three illustrations Henry used for the same poem about Betsey. *Courtesy of the Collection of Brewster Memorial Library/Essex County Historical Society.*

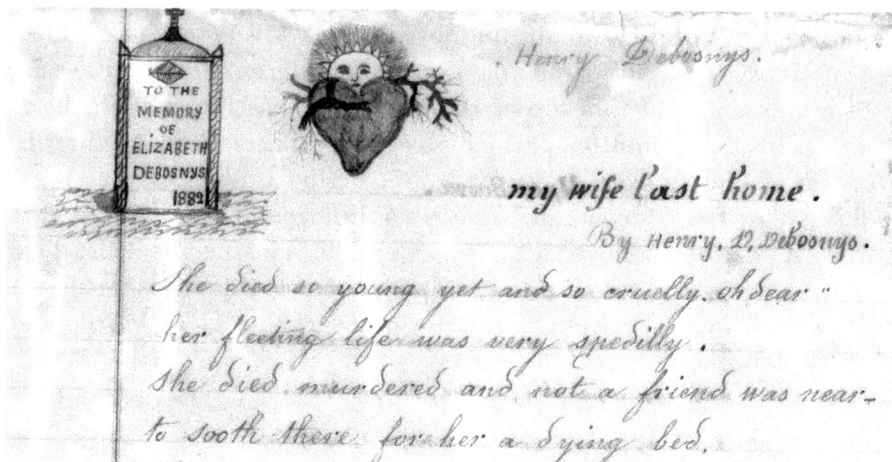

my wife last home.

By Henry. D. Debosnys.

She died so young yet and so cruelly. oh dear

her fleeting life was very spedilly.

she died. murdered and not a friend was near

to sooth there for her a dying bed.

Another of three illustrations Henry used for the same poem about Betsey. *Courtesy of the Collection of Brewster Memorial Library/Essex County Historical Society.*

Grant her to touch this one boon's blissful goal
And take all else that make life worth the living
And leave her destitute; then take her soul,
Her children cry out ceaselessly for blessings,
Yes! Night and day I heard their prayers arise—
To thee, Oh gods they lift up hands beseeching,
The whole round earth is shuddering with their sighs.
The stars keep on in their stately course,
Never minding a word of what they said
All of them still silent are shining bright.
But poor children, your mother, she's dead?
Oh gods eternal! My poor wife, for her better;
I ask no other boon of they blessed hands;
I care not if I starve, low in the gutter
If thou take my wife, with thee in they blessed land.

—*To the Memory of Elizabeth Debosnys*
August 10, 1882
By her husband Henry Debosnys

TREASURE IN THE ATTIC

A little word in kindness spoken
A motion or a tear
Has often healed the heart that's broken
And made a friend sincere
Then deem it not an idle thing
A pleasant word to speak.
The face you wear, the thoughts you bring
A heart may heal or break.
          —*Henry Debosnys, circa 1883*

Shortly before his execution, Henry gave a twenty-six-page collection of historical and artistic sketches, prose and poetry to an older woman who paid him a visit in jail shortly before his execution, and she kept that collection to herself—only sharing the "gift" with her family. When she died in 1917 at the age of ninety-three, her granddaughter, Mrs. Nellie Turner, formerly of Elizabethtown and Altona, found the documents and kept them, storing them away in her attic for many years, until her daughter asked to borrow them. It wasn't until September 10, 1957, when Mrs. Turner read Robert Hall's article about the case in the *Press-Republican*, that "it all came back" to her, she said. She had a whole stack of authentic original documents created by Henry Debosnys! So she called her daughter and had them returned to her at once. Then she wrote to the *Press-Republican* to share her personal knowledge regarding the case.

Mrs. Turner said that her grandmother had told her about cordial conversations she shared with Henry while he was in jail. He told her, "Lady, they have an innocent man here. They claimed I murdered my wife, and I did not." When the woman asked him how Betsey's rings happened to end up in his possession after her body was found, he said that her fingers were swelling on the trip, so she took the rings off and gave them to him to put in his pockets. At one point, Mrs. Turner's grandmother complimented Henry on his white shirt and asked how he kept it so clean and crisp in jail. He told her that he washed the shirts himself, and when they were just about dry, he rubbed them over the hot stove pipe that went up through his cell, effectively ironing out the wrinkles. Another memorable question and answer: How did he make the flowers he drew on the tombstones in his drawings red? To that, he indulged himself and had a little fun with the matronly woman. He told her that there were a lot of flies in his cell, so he killed them and dipped a pointed stick in their blood to acquire the red color. (However, the blood of insects is not red.)

For the kindness she showed to a lonely prisoner who badly needed a friend, Henry offered Mrs. Turner's grandmother his collection of the poetry he had penned, along with drawings and several cryptograms. He wouldn't need them where he was going, and rather than let the authorities destroy them or make a mockery of his talent, he would determine who got what and when. It was the only thing left in his control. After Nellie Turner wrote to the *Press-Republican* offering glimpses of Henry that had never been reported, she wrote a letter on September 17, 1957, to Harry MacDougal at the county courthouse telling him of the prized documents she had in her possession and asking if he knew of "some museum or place" that would be interested in buying them. For three-quarters of a century, nobody had had the opportunity to research Henry's creations and try to determine his identity.

Today, the original documents from Mrs. Turner and others, like Elsie Taylor of Florida and Frances Scheid of California, have found a home in an exhibit focused entirely on Debosnys at the Adirondack History Center Museum in Elizabethtown. Mr. Scheid provided the museum with the jail's original Autographs album that his father, Ben Pond, acquired when he was a young "turnkey" working at the jail during Henry's incarceration. The album contains a number of exquisite drawings and notes Henry added to those that had been left by prisoners before him. Mrs. Taylor wrote to the museum in 1991 and provided them with even more documents from the infamous prisoner. She said that her mother-in-law's mother had worked at the hotel next to the jail where Henry was held and that Sheriff Jenkins had given her the papers on which Henry had jotted down his biographical timeline, along with a piece of the rope used at his execution. How many more "Debosnys originals" are floating around out there? If you're reading this and believe you have something Henry created, please consider donating it to the Adirondack History Center Museum so that everything can be kept safely in one place. Now, then…about those cryptograms.

THE SECRET CODE

As if Debosnys wasn't a hard-enough nut to crack—with the assumed name, savant-like intellect and incredible life story—he had to throw a few impressive crypto-pictograms into the mix before he departed this world, just to keep us guessing. "Cryptology" comes from the Greek *kryptos* and *logos*, meaning "hidden word." Historically, especially in the military, cryptology has been used to send secret messages to specific receivers. During the two world wars, for example, Germany invented the famous "Enigma" encryption device, which was capable of creating what the Germans believed was an impenetrable cryptographic cipher. But during the Second World War, Allied "code breakers" were able to crack the cipher of the rotor machine, thus intercepting secret messages that aided the war effort. Secret societies, like the Knights Templar and the Freemasons, have long used codes, symbols and puzzling pictographs to communicate, as well, in an effort to prevent outsiders from understanding their inner workings. Pity the ousted Freemason who divulged the society's secrets.

Henry's cryptograms contained numerous Masonic symbols, like the square and compass, the gavel and the sun. Interestingly, every time he drew the square and compass—the most identifiable symbol of the Freemasons—it was upside down. This was not by accident. Henry was a stickler for detail in his drawings and would never make such a mistake. Could the reversed square and compass be a secret to his identity? Was he telling us that he had been cast out of the Freemasons or that he failed to show restraint, forgetting to "square his actions by the square of virtue," like the symbol reminds Masons to do?

This page and opposite: Parts one and two of an unsolved combination cryptogram/pictogram created by Debosnys. *Courtesy of the Collection of Brewster Memorial Library/Essex County Historical Society.*

106

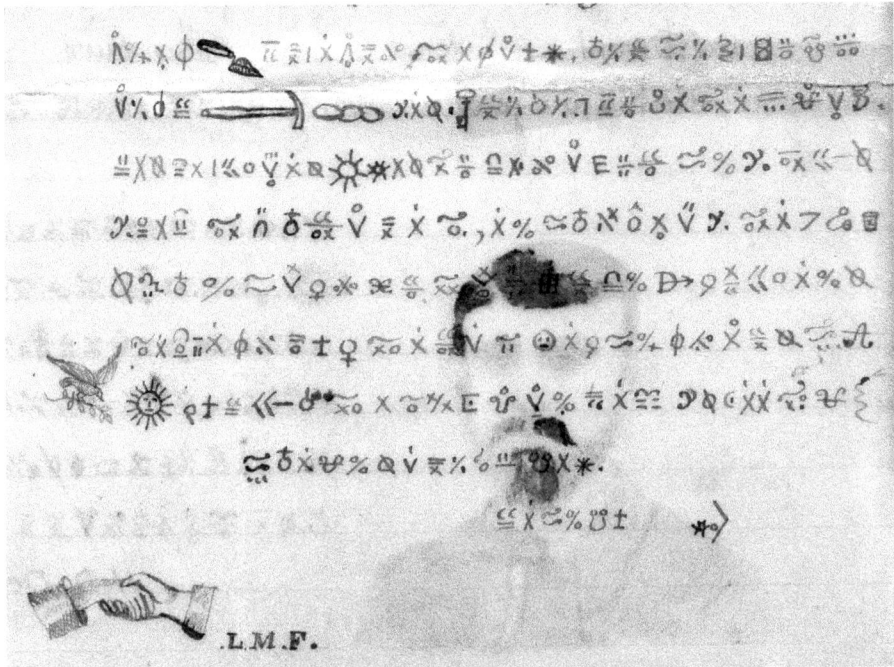

.L.M.F.

Beyond the symbols drawn in his cryptograms, Henry made other references to Freemasonry. For example, in his poem, "Poor Henru—My Last Voyage and My Adieu," he wrote, "For my son, whom I leave in this moment like a shadow of my life, will not be initiated into the first degree." The first degree of what? My guess is the first degree initiation into Freemasonry. At the bottom of one cryptogram, he drew the secret handshake used during the initiation of the First Degree (or Entered Apprentice) that is known as the "Boaz," or "grip of an Entered Apprentice Mason."

Henry had told reporters that the cipher with which he had created his cryptograms was being "widely used" in Europe at the time. Did it have to do with French Freemasonry? Or was it a secret code to which he had access during one of the many battles he fought? Cryptograms were apparently as "hot" then as they are today (think *The Da Vinci Code* and *National Treasure*). Was Henry's repeated use of a reversed "square and compass" a veiled confession that he had a falling out with the Order? Had he become an "anti-Mason," like writer Edgar Allan Poe (according to some)? Conspiracy theorists even suggest that Poe didn't die of unknown causes, as has been widely reported, but that he was murdered at the age of forty for making his misgivings about Freemasonry increasingly public in pieces like "The

A Debosnys cryptogram followed by a French poem. *Courtesy of the Collection of Brewster Memorial Library/Essex County Historical Society.*

Cask of Amontillado" and "Mellonta Tauta." The latter was about George Washington, who laid the cornerstone of the United States Capitol while wearing full Masonic garb, as depicted in a famous painting of that event. The day that Poe died, he was found wandering on the streets of Baltimore delirious and in dire need of medical assistance. He was wearing clothing that did not belong to him and was too incoherent to understand. News articles of the time called the cause of death "cerebral inflammation" by unknown etiology, but rumors have long circulated that he was beaten about the head and left to die. There's a good chance that Henry had studied the life and works of Poe, whose macabre pieces influenced literature around the world, while attending the elite Superior Normal School in Paris in 1858. If so, he surely learned about Poe's cryptograms. In 1839, Poe released two cryptograms under an alias. One was finally cracked in 1992…more than a century and a half after it first appeared. The other has remained unsolved to this day. I wonder if Henry emulated Edgar Allan Poe, with his dark stories and poems and clever use of cryptograms and with his courageous stand against Freemasonry.

If you'll recall, Henry's biography briefly described an incident during the Franco-Prussian War when he was sentenced to be shot at the start of the Paris Commune. In his words:

Colonel Henry stayed at Marseilles until after the bombardment of the Prefecture of the Police by the fort St. Nicholas and Notre-Dame de la Garde, and the surrender of Gaston Cremieux, the chief of the Commune of Marseilles; then returned to Paris with 400 of his men—some of them volunteered in the regular army at Versailles, some at St. Claude. Lived with his father in Paris during the Commune and had 400 guns in his care which he refused to give to the members of the Commune. He was [threatened] to be shot by the generals Cluseret and Rosselle, in company of a man named Delescluze, for refusing to take part in the Commune and deliver his guns. Colonel Henry made some wood boxes and packed the guns and put them away in the cellar of his house where the regular army of Versailles found them upon their entrance into Paris. Colonel Henry was arrested and sent to Versailles; was tried and sentenced to be shot the same day of the sentence, but he made his escape through a platoon of 30 bayonets and went back to Paris to his father; took 3,000 francs and then took the cars for Brussels, Belgium, where he remained until all the errors of the sentence were corrected. He then returned to Paris and went to Havre de Grace where he embarked on board the Cimbria for New York in June. His wife, Mrs. Judith Debosnys, died in July and her body was sent to France to be buried in her family vault; the father of the wife accompanied the body to France.

According to a Wikipedia article ("History of Freemasonry in France"), the Paris Commune proved to be a pivotal moment, not just for Debosnys but for Parisian Freemasons, as well. In 1870, there were eighteen thousand Freemasons of the Grand Orient of France. When the events of the Paris Commune began in March 1871, Parisian Freemasons were asked to step up to the plate and support the Commune by setting up Masonic banners along the city's walls. If those banners were desecrated by anti-Commune forces, the Masons were to take their revenge on those forces. (And Henry, who I'm increasingly convinced was a Parisian Freemason based on symbols he used and things he said, was on the forefront of the *anti*-Commune forces, which must have put him in quite a pickle.) On April 29, 1871, thousands of Parisian Freemasons like Vallès and Reclus stood behind their banners to demonstrate against Versailles forces.

Talks between two representatives of the Commune failed. Divided, they fell. The Paris Commune was soundly defeated. The Grand Orient, under whom all French Freemasons act, was not happy with the Parisian Freemasons, because they acted apart from provincial French Freemasons who did not support the Paris Commune. So the Grand Orient officially disavowed the actions of the Parisian Freemasons. Because Henry had refused to send the four hundred guns he had stashed in his father's basement to Delecluse, a supporter of the Commune, he became an enemy of the Commune (and Freemasons). He also became an enemy of the Versailles forces when they discovered the hidden weapons in the cellar. He was sentenced to be shot but managed to escape to Belgium before returning to America. Could Henry's "Delecluse" have been the leading Parisian Freemason "Elisee Recluse" mentioned above, who was then banished from France for his political activism after publishing a manifesto in support of the Paris Commune? Was that what he was running from for the rest of his life? Further investigation into this possibility is warranted. I believe the key to his identity lies in that singular, tumultuous episode of French and Masonic history.

The Debosnys papers seem to be a mishmash of many ciphers or a combination of ciphers and symbols. If anyone could pull off creating his own secret cipher, it would be Henry, with his vast knowledge of history, other cultures and multiple languages. To be honest, a lot of the symbols he used remind me of those seen in the "Anthon Transcript" (aka the "Caractors" document), which Palmyra, New York farmer Martin Harris received from Joseph Smith Jr. in 1828. Smith, the founder of the Latter-Day Saints movement, was just eighteen years old when he claimed that

Part one of an unsolved combination cryptogram/pictogram created by Debosnys. *Courtesy of the Collection of Brewster Memorial Library/Essex County Historical Society.*

. Hênêcos Debosnostys .

Stat gravis Entellus, nisuque immotus eodem, corpore tela modo atque oculis vigilantibus exit.

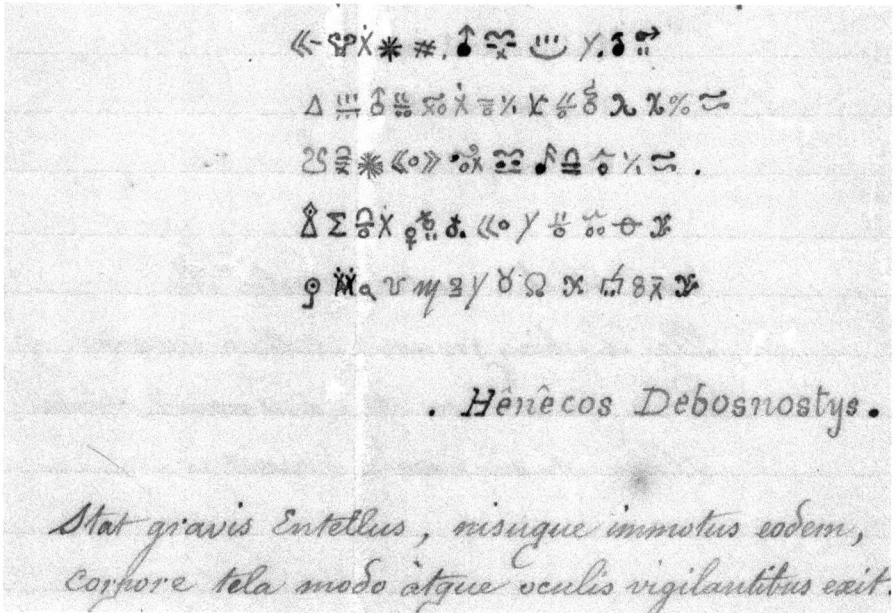

Part two of an unsolved combination cryptogram/pictogram created by Debosnys. *Courtesy of the Collection of Brewster Memorial Library/Essex County Historical Society.*

the transcript was allegedly revealed to him on gold plates by angels. I've spent countless hours trying to decipher Henry's cryptograms. They seem to include a mixture of Freemasonry symbols and an unknown cipher or combination of ancient ciphers. There are similar characters in the ancient Phoenician, Proto-Sinaitic and Aramaic scripts, to some degree. I've also tried using frequency of letters (or, in this case, frequency of characters) as a method of determining what letter each character might represent, but to no avail. With a manuscript deadline for another book looming, I'm counting on you, the reader, to find the answer that has eluded me throughout my extensive research. I feel that I've gotten so close to resolving this enigma that I can almost taste it. Unfortunately, I have other mysteries to solve and deadlines to meet.

Here is Henry's supposed translation of the cipher above in Greek. The cipher was on one side of the foolscap, with what he called the "Greek translation" on the other side.

(GreeK translation.)

ΕΠΙ ῥοδίνοις ταῖ γου,

Τμίος ποτ' ἀ μελιςης

'Ιλαρος γελων εκιτο,

Μεθυωντε και λυριζων

Αμφι αυτον οξ δ' ερωτες

'Απαλοι συνεχορευσαν,

Εποιει, ψυχης οἴσους·

Ο δε λευκα πορφυροισι

Κρινα συν ῥοδοισι πλεξας,

Εφιλει σεφ ων γεροντα·

Η δε Θεαων αυασσα,

ΣΟΦΙΗ ποτ' εξ Ολ υμπου

Δε . . Εσπρω σ' Ανακρεοντα,

Δ . . . Ευ . . . τοῖς . . .

Γ πορειδ ι . . . . . ·

Σοφε, δ' ὡς Ανακρεοντα

Τον σοφωτατον ἁπαντων,

Καλεουσιν οἱ σοφισαι,

Τι γερων, τεον Βιον μεν

Ωδε Βιατον γαληνον   ?

Greek translation of the previous cryptogram, written on the back of same document.
Courtesy of the Collection of Brewster Memorial Library/Essex County Historical Society.

OH, HENRY!

In a 1977 *Press-Republican* article called "'Ghost' of deBosney to Get New Environment" by M.B. Allen, the correspondent reported that upon verification of Henry's death—and after the brief, customary public viewing—Dr. Pattison took the corpse and removed the flesh down to the bone before burying all but the skeleton in a shallow grave twenty feet from the south bank of Lee Park (where a new bridge was being built in 1977). Pattison, the article said, had arranged to have a gravestone carver named Andrew Daniels make a simple slab to designate the deceased's grave. However, the grave marker was never put in place, for some unknown reason. A rumor persisted that Henry's ghost was known to make occasional appearances at the site of his unmarked grave. After wiring the bones back together like a puzzle, recreating Henry's skeleton, Pattison either hung it in the loft of his barn or kept it in his office as a model for scientific study for several years, depending on which source you reference.

In 1933, Ticonderoga's Dr. H.E. Douglass told the *Sentinel* that he and another medical student, whom he didn't name, purchased the skeleton for medical purposes. Perhaps Pattison was the other doctor to whom he referred. Douglass said that he and his companion visited Henry in jail a few days prior to his execution, and Henry signed a bill of sale for fifteen dollars, using the money to buy gifts (the candy and peanuts he reportedly purchased?) for the sheriff's children. The night they transported Henry's remains from the jail in Elizabethtown to the apartment in Westport, where they "dissected" it, was "the darkest night [he] ever experienced." With the

Debosnys poem and illustration. *Courtesy of the Collection of Brewster Memorial Library/Essex County Historical Society.*

corpse laid out across a seat in the back of their wagon, they bumped into another wagon as it passed by them heading toward Elizabethtown. They feared the worst, having been forewarned that a doctor from Ausable Forks was mighty upset that Henry had accepted the students' offer of fifteen dollars, when he had offered fifty dollars for the remains. They were told that he might "resort to drastic measures" to get what he believed should have been his. Luckily, the two medical students didn't need to wield the guns they were carrying, since the person in the other wagon was definitely not a doctor from Ausable, so both parties continued on their ways.

Regardless of who actually purchased and took possession of the body—Pattison or Douglass—when they had no further use for the skeleton, it was donated to the science department of the Westport School District. However, according to Billie Allen in a *Valley News* "Mountain Laurel" column in 1973, the skeleton was manhandled and used as a prop in pranks (especially around Halloween time) so often that it eventually fell apart and was disposed of. All that remained at the school was the skull. But in 1961,

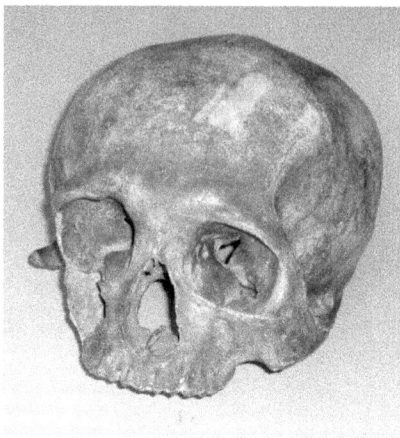

Henry's skull from the Collection of Adirondack History Center Museum/ Essex County Historical Society. *Photo by author.*

with the encouragement of several determined individuals, like Allen and Elizabeth Twa, the school donated the skull to the Adirondack History Center Museum in Elizabethtown. And that's where a little piece of Henry remains to this day, along with the actual noose used at his execution, a ticket to same and other fascinating Debosnys-related objects. Some believe that Henry's ghost even haunts the museum, when it's not busy haunting its grave site or the Old Essex County Courthouse at 7551 Court Street in Elizabethtown. Today the old courthouse is used as the Essex County Government Center and no longer holds court, since a new courthouse has been built at the far end of the courthouse grounds. It does, however, hold the County Manager's Office, the board of supervisors chambers and a server room for the county Information Systems Department.

Henry was hanged in front of the Government Center, where the last thing his mortal eyes saw before the black hood was drawn over his head and the noose tightened around his neck was a massive crowd of people anxiously awaiting his demise. Does he now haunt the spot where his fate was sealed by the sentence Judge Landon handed down—the spot where it was determined that he only had fifty-one days to live? I wouldn't say that the Government Center is haunted, but I did dig up one incident that made me wonder. In the board of supervisors' public minutes for the county's Personnel & Administration Committee's May 2008 meeting that were posted online, an isolated incident occurred in the locked Information Systems Department server room in the building. At that meeting, County Manager Daniel Palmer said:

> We have a Charter fiber line that runs from here down to the Public Safety Building, last Sunday it did go down. This is a leased line from Charter Communications, it's monitored 24/7...It turned out that it was a broken whip line and what happens is when your primary connection comes into the building from the connection to a switch, there is a small, thin fiber-optic line that connects from one to the other, and one of them had gotten physically

broken. I have no idea how it got broken in a locked Information Systems Department, in a locked server room, but it did…it was a physically broken whip line.

Moriah town supervisor Tom Scozzafava asked if it looked like it was intentional or vandalism and quipped, "Do we have ghosts running around the building? If nobody is getting into that room, I mean, is it being investigated?" Palmer's response was, "I don't know how to investigate it, Tom. I honestly don't." So Scozzafava suggested, "You might want to think about having [a camera] in there. How does a line 'just break'?" Palmer said that it's possible that a mouse could get on it but that "there were no chew marks or anything like that," and he added that it wasn't due to the age of the line, because they were all brand new. "It is a little bit disconcerting to me," Palmer admitted. Scozzafava told me in an e-mail on December 13, 2008, "We never did find out what happened to the line." If it's paranormal in nature, which I'm not saying it is, wouldn't an obvious candidate for the ghostly culprit be one of the few men hanged on those very grounds?

It gets better. When I visited the Adirondack History Center Museum in Elizabethtown (just a three-minute walk from the Government Center) in September 2009 to get images for this book, we had a little incident. Actually, we had a couple of little incidents. Jenifer Kuba, the assistant director and archivist/curator, set me up at her desk in the Brewster Library with a box containing the original documents Henry created in jail so that I could determine which ones I would like images of for this book. These artifacts are rarely taken off the shelf anymore, because all of the images have been digitized for anyone wishing to see them—that way the delicate originals can be preserved.

Shortly after I began to leaf through the pages that have survived 127 years, I heard a buzz (like electrical wires sparking), and the overhead lights in the room turned off and then back on. Fortunately, I wasn't alone in the room. Jenifer and Margaret Gibbs, the director, were sitting at the conference table in the middle of the library talking to a couple of ladies. They looked at me when it happened to see if I'd lost anything on the computer, and just as I was about to respond, we heard the same thing again, and again the lights went off and on. Margaret and Jenifer both said that they've never seen that happen in the library before. They went out in the hallway to ask people in other rooms if their lights had dimmed, but it had only happened in the library where I happened to be looking through Henry's papers. There were other unusual electrical problems that day, as well. The copier, with which

Jenifer was copying documents from my files to add to the museum's, was running much slower than usual, she told me. And then the computer shut down. A few moments later, Margaret came into the room and said not to worry and that it wasn't Henry (as we were all suspecting by then), because it was a "county-wide outage." That's when I chuckled and told her about the May 2008 incident with the fiber-optic line tripping at the Government Center where Henry was convicted and hanged. What are the odds that on the very day I visited the museum to get information and images for a book about Henry Debosnys the lights would turn off in the library for apparently the first time ever and that the fiber-optic cable that provides Internet service to the county would trip for only the second time in two years?

It would make sense for Henry to haunt the museum. It has his skull on display. I've included the museum's ghost stories in previous books, most recently my *Big Book of New York Ghost Stories*. The first memorable incident occurred in the museum's library, where the lighting incident happened, when nobody was there. Margaret told me:

> *The* [newspaper] *article was in the out tray of the copier when we arrived in the morning, but there was nothing in the copier—on the glass of the copier where the original article would have to be to make a copy. We did not know how it was copied. When we held it up and asked the other staff in the library if anyone had copied it, everyone said no; and at that same moment, the power went out in the building and surrounding area.*

Not long after that, an intern named Jessie Olcott was in the basement with another young lady when they noticed "a face in the glass on the Crown Point table on the floor below." Nobody responded when they called out, so they ran upstairs to get Margaret to help them find the person. Whoever it was couldn't have walked past them without being noticed, yet somehow they had. Recalling the image of Henry's face on the newspaper that had been mysteriously photocopied in the library just days before, they realized that it was the same face they had seen reflecting off the glass on the table. Jessie was asked to research the crime and create an exhibit regarding Henry Debosnys. Lo and behold, that's when she learned that her ancestor, Deputy Sheriff S.S. Olcott, had not only arrested Henry for murder, but he had also pulled the hood over his head during the execution.

Margaret said that the most frightening incident she and Jessie experienced happened a few days before the Debosnys exhibit was slated to open. Jessie told me:

Debosnys exhibit at the Adirondack History Center Museum/Essex County Historical Society. *Photo by author.*

I was turning off the upstairs lights for the receptionists. When I went to the last room on the right, I went to turn off the lights, which are special in this room, because they are like breakers that you have to turn off one by one. Well, I didn't get to turn out even one light before they all went out one by one, all by themselves! The switchbox was in a room across from the library, and when the incident occurred, the museum director was right out in the hall, so she witnessed it as well. She went to the switchbox to see if it would happen again, but it didn't. She said, "You have to switch one on at a time. It would be impossible to switch them all on at the same time [with just two hands], *or at least very awkward and difficult."*

It seems that in death, as in life, Henry has bounced from place to place determined to leave his mark wherever he goes. At the Adirondack History Center Museum, when something happens that can't be explained—like the lights turning off in the library as I thumbed through the original documents Henry created—he gets blamed for it. In fact, his latest tricks prompted one of the members of the staff to suggest that I name the

Debosnys self-portrait in the jailhouse Autographs book. *Courtesy of the Collection of Adirondack History Center Museum/Essex County Historical Society.*

book *Oh, Henry!* since those were the words the three of us uttered nearly in unison when his shameless antics became obvious that day. Museum personnel have noticed a definite pattern of Henry "acting up" whenever someone is talking about him or working on the exhibit bearing his name. So it really came as no surprise to anyone that he would get excited when I visited that day, considering the mission I was on. In that regard, I hope I've shed a little light on the strange story of Henry Debosnys's life and taken a new generation one or two steps closer to determining who this Adirondack enigma really was.

BIBLIOGRAPHY

CORRESPONDENCE

Allen, Billie. Letter to James Bailey, August 16, 1973.
———. Unpublished news column for "Mountain Laurel." *Valley News*, August 22, 1973.
Davis, William F. "The DeBosnys Murder Case," undated, but after 1961.
Hall, Robert. Notes to unknown, 1957.
Scheid, Frances. Letter to Mrs. Casselman. Adirondack Center Museum, June 16, 1983.
Taylor, Elsie B. Letter to Reid S. Larson. Essex County Historical Society, October 1, 1991.
Turner, Nellie. Letter to Harry MacDougle, September 17, 1957.
———. Letter to *Press Republican*, September 1957.

NEWSPAPERS

Allen, Billie. "Mountain Laurel: Essex County's Most Famous Murder." *Valley News*, July 5, 1973.
———. "Mountain Laurel: Explanation, Please!" *Valley News*, July 26, 1973.
———. "Mountain Laurel." *Valley News*, August 9, 1973.
Allen, M.B. "Ghost of deBosney to Get New Environment." *Press-Republican*, July 22, 1977.
Clayton, David. "Killer Hanged 100 Years Ago Today." *Press-Republican*, April 27, 1983.

BIBLIOGRAPHY

Essex County Republican. "The Gallows in Essex County. Second Execution in its History. Henry Debosnys." May 3, 1883.

———. "Story of Essex County Second Execution." April 21, 1933.

Hall, Robert. "Essex County Murders Still Remembered After 75 Years." *Press-Republican*, September 10, 1957.

Malone Palladium. "A Murderer's Strange Story." November 23, 1882.

New York Times. "A Remarkable Man Hanged." April 28, 1883.

———. "A Wife's Fearful Death." August 6, 1882.

Plattsburgh Sentinel. "Accident at the Mines." December 16, 1870.

———. "The Career of DeBosnys." April 27, 1883.

———. "An Essex County Crime. Henry Debosnys's Checkered Career and How He Murdered His Third Wife and Paid the Penalty." May 3, 1901.

———. "The Essex County Murderer. The Missing Colored Cook Found at Philadelphia." Undated [summer 1882].

———. "The Gallows in Essex County. Second Execution in its History. Henry Debosnys." May 4, 1883.

———. Local note on Debosnys regarding oyer and terminer, September 15, 1882.

———. Local note on Debosnys regarding request to French Consul, August 18, 1882.

———. Local note on Debosnys regarding suspected drowning of wife in Philadelphia, January 12, 1883.

———. Local notes regarding murder, August 4, 1882.

———. "The Murder of Mrs. Wells." August 11, 1882.

———. "The Trial of DeBosnys." March 9, 1883.

Plattsburgh Telegram. "Cold Blooded Murder." August 3, 1882.

Porter, Marjorie. "Split Rock Historical Lore." *Essex County Republican*, August 27, 1957.

Post & Gazette. "Debosnys History. [Continued from last week]." April 19, 1883.

———. "Executed! Henry Delectnack Debosnys (So Called) Pays the Penalty for Murder." April 26, 1883.

———. "Henry Delectnack Debosnys (So Called)." April 25, 1901.

———. "He reported the Debosnys Murder Trial." May 9, 1901.

———. Local note regarding Debosnys, post execution, May 3, 1883.

———. Miscellaneous regarding Debosnys's interview, April 12, 1883.

———. "Murder." August 3, 1882.

———. "The Trial of Henry Delecnac Debosnys for the Murder of His Wife, Betsey Wells." March 8, 1883.

———. "The Trial of Henry Delecnac Debosnys for the Murder of His Wife, Betsey Wells [Cont'd.]." March 15, 1883.

Schwarz-Kopf, Rebecca. "Henry Debosnys, and the wife he murdered." *Lake Champlain Weekly*, May 16, 2001.

Sentinel. Local note on Debosnys regarding "not guilty" plea, December 22, 1882.

Ticonderoga Sentinel. Local note regarding Debosnys document, May 18, 1933.

BIBLIOGRAPHY

———. "More Sidelights on County's Last Hanging." May 11, 1933.

Valley News. "Essex County's Most Famous Murder." March 8, 1962.

BOOKS

Horne, Alistair. *The Fall of Paris: The Siege and the Commune 1870–71.* New York: Penguin, 2007.

King, David A. *The Ciphers of the Monks: A Forgotten Number-Notation of the Middle Ages.* Stuttgart, Germany: Franz Steiner Verlag, 2001.

Mackey, Albert Gallatin. *Encyclopedia of Freemasonry and Its Kindred Sciences.* Chicago: Masonic History Company, 1912.

MacNulty, W. Kirk. *Freemasonry: A Journey through Ritual and Symbol.* London: Thames & Hudson Ltd., 1991.

Murray, T. Douglas, trans. *Jeanne d'Arc, Maid of Orleans, Deliverer of France.* London: William Heinemann, 1907.

Revai, Cheri. "Adirondack History Center Museum." *The Big Book of New York Ghost Stories.* Mechanicsburg, PA: Stackpole Books Inc., 2009.

———. "The Skull." *More Haunted Northern New York.* Utica, NY: North Country Books, 2003.

Storey, Henry Wilson. *History of Cambria County, Pennsylvania.* Vol. 2. New York: Lewis Publishing Company, 1907.

ONLINE SOURCES

"Adirondack History Center Museum." Essex County Historical Society. www.adkhistorycenter.org/pla/planavisit.html.

"The Alphabet in Heiroglyphs, Page 2." Heiroglyph Alphabet. http://caesarcoinmarket.com/heiroglyphalphab.html.

"Battle of the Little Bighorn." Wikipedia, the free encyclopedia. http://en.wikipedia.org/wiki/Battle_of_the_Little_Bighorn.

Burkle, Brother William Steve, KT. "The Freemasons' Magic Square." Speculation on the Symbol of the Square and Compasses. www.freemasons-freemasonry.com/freemasons_magic_square.html.

"Cimbria (1867)." Palmer List of Merchant Vessels—C. www.geocities.com/mppraetorius/com-ci.htm.

"Civil War Veterans' Card File, 1861–1866." Pennsylvania State Archives. http://www.digitalarchives.state.pa.us/archive.asp?view=ArchiveIndexes&ArchiveID=17.

Cope, Dorian. "21st May 1871—La Semaine Sanglante Begins." On This Deity. http://doriancope.blogspot.com/2009/05/21st-may-1871-la-semaine-sanglante.html.

"Corsica." Wikipedia, the free encyclopedia. http://en.wikipedia.org/wiki/Corsica.

Davy. "The Insurrection in Paris, by an Englishman." Project Gutenberg. http://www.gutenberg.org/dirs/1/9/9/1/19912/19912-8.txt.

"Edgar Allan Poe." Wikipedia, the free encyclopedia. http://en.wikipedia.org/wiki/Edgar_Allan_Poe.

"Edmond François Valentin About." Wikipedia, the free encyclopedia. http://en.wikipedia.org/wiki/Edmond_Fran%C3%A7ois_Valentin_About.

"Greek." Ancient Scripts. www.ancientscripts.com/greek.html.

"History of Freemasonry in France." Wikipedia, the free encyclopedia. http://en.wikipedia.org/wiki/History_of_Freemasonry_in_France.

Howard, Robert. "United States Presidents and the Illuminati/Masonic Power Structure." The Forbidden Knowledge. www.theforbiddenknowledge.com/hardtruth/uspresidentasmasons.htm.

Kallis, Stephen A., Jr. "Codes and Ciphers." Radio Days. http://www.otr.com/ciphers.shtml

"Kim Peek." Wikipedia, the free encyclopedia. http://en.wikipedia.org/wiki/Kim_Peek.

"Letter frequencies." Wikipedia, the free encyclopedia. http://en.wikipedia.org/wiki/Lettter_frequencies.

"Mad as a Hatter." Corrosion Doctors. http://corrosion-doctors.org/Elements-Toxic/Mercury-mad-hatter.htm.

"Mercury (element)." Wikipedia, the free encyclopedia. http://en.wikipedia.org/wiki/Mercury_(element).

"Northern New York Historical Newspapers." Northern New York Library Network. http://news.nnyln.net.

Pelling, Nick. "The Anthon Transcript." Cipher Mysteries. www.ciphermysteries.com/2008/05/13/the-anthon-transcript.

———. "The E.A. Poe Cryptographic Challenge." Cipher Mysteries. www.ciphermysteries.com/2008/05/13/the-e-a-poe-cryptographic-challenge.

"Proto-Sinaitic." Ancient Scripts. www.ancientscripts.com/protosinaitic.html.

"Reformed Egyptian." Wikipedia, the free encyclopedia. http://en.wikipedia.org/wiki/Anthon_transcript.

"Savant syndrome." Wikipedia, the free encyclopedia. http://en.wikipedia.org/wiki/Savant_syndrome.

Smith, Derek J. "Cryptology and the Electric Telegraph (1853–1865)." Codes and Ciphers in History, Part 2—1853 to 1917. http://www.smithsrisca.demon.co.uk/crypto-middle.html.

"The 10 Most Insane Medical Practices in History." Cracked. www.cracked.com/article_15669_10-most-insane-medical-practices-in-history.html.

"Zodiac Killer." Answers.com. www.answers.com/topic/zodiac-killer-1?cat=entertainment.

Index

ABOUT THE AUTHOR

Author Cheri Farnsworth and Coco. *Photo by daughter Jamie Revai.*

Cheri Farnsworth has written the following titles (some under the name of Cheri Revai): *Haunted Northern New York* (2002), *More Haunted Northern New York* (2003), *Still More Haunted Northern New York* (2004), *Haunted Massachusetts: Ghosts & Strange Phenomena of the Bay State* (2005), *Haunted New York: Ghosts & Strange Phenomena of the Empire State* (2005), *Haunted Connecticut: Ghosts & Strange Phenomena of the Constitution State* (2006), *Haunted New York City: Ghosts & Strange Phenomena of the Big Apple* (2008), *The Big Book of New York Ghost Stories* (2009), *Haunted Hudson Valley* (2010), *North Country Ghosts* (TBR Fall 2010), *Murder and Mayhem in Northern New York* (TBR Fall 2010) and *Alphabet Murders* (TBR Fall 2010).

While she has enjoyed researching the connection between history and the paranormal for the past several years, a new chapter of her life has begun with *Adirondack Enigma*, the author's first book on true crime. Farnsworth lives in Northern New York with her husband, daughters and a houseful of pets.

www.ingramcontent.com/pod-product-compliance
Lightning Source LLC
Chambersburg PA
CBHW070348100426
42812CB00005B/1455